SO-CAY-848

NEW GENDER MAINSTREAMING SERIES ON DEVELOPMENT ISSUES

Gender in Primary and Secondary Education

A Handbook for Policy-makers and Other Stakeholders

Ramya Subrahmanian

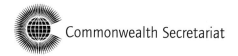

Commonwealth Secretariat

Commonwealth Secretariat
Marlborough House, Pall Mall
London SW1Y 5HX
United Kingdom

© Commonwealth Secretariat 2007

All rights reserved. No part of this
publication may be reproduced,
stored in a retrieval system, or
transmitted in any form or by any
means, electronic or mechanical,
including photocopying, recording
or otherwise without the
permission of the publisher.

Published by the Commonwealth
Secretariat
Edited and designed by Wayzgoose
Cover design by Pen & Ink Book
Co Ltd
Index compiled by Indexing
Specialists (UK) Ltd.
Printed by Hobbs the Printers

Views and opinions expressed in
this publication are the responsibility
of the author and should in no way
be attributed to the institutions to
which she is affiliated, or to the
Commonwealth Secretariat.

Wherever possible, the
Commonwealth Secretariat uses
paper sourced from sustainable
forests or from sources that
minimise a destructive impact on
the environment.

Cover photo credit:
© www.JohnBirdsall.co.uk

Copies of this publication may be
obtained from
The Publications Section
Commonwealth Secretariat
Marlborough House, Pall Mall
London SW1Y 5HX
United Kingdom
Tel: +44 (0)20 7747 6342
Fax: +44 (0)20 7839 9081
E-mail:
publications@commonwealth.int

Web: www.thecommonwealth.org/
publications

A catalogue record for this
publication is available from the
British Library.

ISBN: 978-0-85092-864-8

Other titles in the New Gender Mainstreaming Series on Development Issues

Gender Mainstreaming in HIV/AIDS: Taking a Multisectoral Approach,
2002

*Gender Mainstreaming in the Health Sector: Experiences in
Commonwealth Countries*, 2002

Promoting an Integrated Approach to Combat Gender Based Violence,
2002

*Engendering Budgets: A Practitioners' Guide to Understanding and
Implementing Gender-responsive Budgets*, 2003

*Gender Mainstreaming in Poverty Eradication and the Millennium
Development Goals*, 2003

Gender Mainstreaming in the Multilateral Trading System, 2003

Integrated Approaches to Eliminating Gender-based Violence, 2003
(non-priced publication)

Mainstreaming Informal Employment and Gender in Poverty Reduction,
2004

Gender Mainstreaming in Conflict Transformation, 2005

Mainstreaming Gender in Social Protection for the Informal Economy,
2007

About the Author

Ramya Subrahmanian is a former Fellow at the Institute of Development Studies at the University of Sussex, UK, and is currently Social Policy Specialist at UNICEF India.

Contents

Foreword   vii

Abbreviations   ix

Executive Summary   xi

1. Gender, Education and Development   1

     Achievements and Gaps   2
     Why Paying Attention to Gender and Education is   8
     Important
     Conclusion   18

2. Reframing the Education Policy Discourse: 21
     Rights, Capabilities and Empowerment
     Gender Equality in Education: Framing a   22
     Substantive Approach
     Widening the Scope of Gender and Education   26
     Interventions: Towards a Rights-based Approach
     Conclusion   35

3. The Gendered Construction of the Demand for   37
     Girls' Education
     Gender Inequalities and Education   39
     Structural Determinants of Female Disadvantage   43
     in Education
     Reproduction of Labour and its Relationship with   53
     Schooling
     Conclusion   58

4. Supply-side Constraints on Girls' Schooling   59
     Reproducing Society through the Education System   60
     The Schooling Experience: Gender-based Violence   61
     Teachers as Shapers of Gender Equality   63
     The 'Hidden Curriculum'   65
     Boys and Girls in the Classroom: Gender Inequalities   66
     and Learning Outcomes
     Policy Issues   76
     Conclusion   93

5. Policies and Programmes for Promoting Gender-   95
    equitable Schooling
    Lessons from Experience   98
    Conclusion   119

6. Institutional Transformation and Gender   121
    Mainstreaming in Education
    Why Gender Mainstreaming?   122
    Defining Gender Mainstreaming   124
    Strategies for Mainstreaming Gender Equality   127
    Mainstreaming Gender in the New International   136
    Aid *Architecture*
    Conclusion   140

References   143

Index   153

Foreword

The Commonwealth is a voluntary association of 53 states bound by a set of shared values and principles. One of these principles is that every child in the Commonwealth, whether girl or boy, has the right to a quality education. It will take some time for this right to be realised, however, since around 30 million Commonwealth children are not in primary school – and the majority of these are girls.

These statistics drive the Commonwealth's commitment to achieving the two education-related Millennium Development Goals (MDGs): achieving universal primary education by 2015 and eliminating gender disparities in education. Regrettably, an estimated 94 countries worldwide failed to meet the first MDG target of eliminating gender disparities in primary and secondary education by 2005. It has been estimated that if the target had been reached, an additional 6 million girls would now be in school in Commonwealth countries in South Asia.

In addition to the targeted education measures to give girls access to school and ensure that they have a quality learning experience when they get there, the Secretariat is working to implement the *Commonwealth Plan for Gender Equality 2005–2015*. The *Plan*, endorsed in 2005 by all Commonwealth Heads of Government, commits the Commonwealth to improving the social status of girls and women and to putting in place the conditions that will enable them to enrol and stay in school.

After decades of advocacy and targets about the rights of the girl child, and evidence on the economic and social multiplier effects of investing in girls' education, we still have some way to go in eliminating gender inequalities in education. I am therefore very pleased to introduce this excellent handbook for policy-makers on gender mainstreaming in education by Ramya Subrahmanian. As the author notes: 'Large sections of populations – a significant proportion of whom are girls – are locked out of schooling and formal education institutions'.

This book is another quality publication in the Commonwealth Secretariat's series on *Gender Mainstreaming*, and a further step towards enabling all Commonwealth children to take their rightful place in the classroom.

Ann Keeling
Director
Social Transformation Programmes Division

Abbreviations

AFT	Analytical Fast Track
BRAC	Bangladesh Rural Advancement Committee
CEDAW	Convention on the Elimination of All Forms of Discrimination Against Women
CRC	Convention on the Rights of the Child
CWD	Children with Disabilities
DFID	Department for International Development (UK)
ECCE	Early Childhood Care and Education
ECLAC	Economic Commission for Latin America and the Caribbean
EFA	Education for All
EGS	Education Guarantee Scheme
EOC	Equal Opportunities Commission (UK)
FSP	Female Stipend Programme
FTI	Fast Track Initiative
GAD	Gender and Development
GER	Gross Enrolment Ratio
HCT	Human Capital Theory
HIPC	Heavily Indebted Poor Countries
HRW	Human Rights Watch
ICCPR	International Covenant on Civil and Political Rights
ICESCR	International Covenant on Economic, Social and Cultural Rights
IDPs	Internally Displaced Persons
IGT	Intergenerational Transmission
MDGs	Millennium Development Goals
NASSPE	National Association for Single Sex Public Education
NER	Net Enrolment Ratio
NGO	Non-governmental Organisation
NSSO	National Sample Survey Organisation (India)
OECD	Organisation for Economic Co-operation and Development
OECD-DAC	Organisation for Economic Co-operation and Development – Development Assistance Committee
PESP	Primary Education Stipend Programme

PISA	Programme for International Student Assessment
PROBE	Public Report on Basic Education
PRS	Poverty Reduction Strategy
PRSP	Poverty Reduction Strategy Paper
RBA	Rights-based Approach
SAHE	Society for the Advancement of Education
SMC	School Management Committee
SSC	Secondary School Certificate
SWAps	Sector Wide Approaches
UDHR	Universal Declaration of Human Rights
UEE	Universal Elementary Education
UIS	UNESCO Institute for Statistics
UNESCO	United Nations Educational, Scientific and Cultural Organisation
UNGEI	UN Girls' Education Initiative
UNICEF	United Nations Children's Fund
UPE	Universal Primary Education
WEF	World Education Forum
WHO	World Health Organisation
WID	Women in Development

Executive Summary

This handbook on gender mainstreaming in education has been written in the context of rapidly expanding education systems worldwide, and in particular the growing numbers of girls entering school. In this new situation, the issue of gender mainstreaming goes beyond building schools and ensuring access to meeting the challenge of how to sustain these gains. It is now critical to build on the base of rising enrolments to secure the future of education for girls. It is widely accepted that girls' education is a vital piece in the bigger jigsaw puzzle of human development and social change. Thus gender mainstreaming in education must address the more strategic questions of the connections between education and wider development, and the relationships between men and women in a rapidly changing world.

The role of public policy and state action is becoming ever more critical in the face of diversifying systems of educational provision. Increasingly, as diverse providers join governments in trying to meet the spiralling demand for education, the role of the state in managing expectations, setting standards and monitoring quality and equity in education has become a central concern. Gender mainstreaming, as a project which attempts to ensure that all public policies take into account the potential implications of all actions, resource allocations and programmes on women and men, seeks to transform the ways in which public resources and investment are distributed. This means that it is important to pay attention to the ideologies that underlie the formulation and implementation of policies; the biases in the rules and practices that determine how ideas are translated into action; and the allocation of resources so that investment is distributed equitably. The notion of 'the public' goes beyond the state to encompass all actors working together to deliver the public good, including the state, civil society organisations, the private sector, and multilateral and bilateral agencies.

Substantial progress towards closing the gender gap in education has already been made, particularly in primary education. However, in secondary and higher education, in situations where gender parity has been achieved in developing countries, this often reflects class privilege, as the spread of enrolment is not universal. Issues of retention and completion, together with improvements in the quality of education, demand central attention in the policy agenda. Making school environments affordable, safe and well-resourced, and improving the quality of education are critical challenges ahead.

Current levels of female participation in schooling are unprecedented, signalling the success of the strategies that have been employed by governments and international, national and local development agencies to facilitate greater female schooling. However, gaps persist and gains are not yet fully sustainable. To take the movement for girls' education further, new approaches and strategies are required. Three main messages can be drawn from a review of shifting paradigms in thinking about female education.

First, advocacy for education as a whole is necessary for the promotion of girls' education to be sustained. Investment in programmes for girls' education needs to be matched by overall improvements in education systems, particularly in relation to improving the quality of teaching, the curriculum and curriculum transaction. Too often, girls' education is discussed as a distinct set of concerns and is separated from discussion of the reform of education systems as a whole. The two are fundamentally interlinked. Specific measures for improving the enrolment and participation of girls will only succeed if overall policies are pro-equity, pro-poor and pro-marginalised groups.

Second, linkages between education and other investments in human well-being are important. This is particularly true for female education: investment in health, nutrition and employment opportunities is all relevant to girls' education and hence needs to be coherently addressed. Far greater attention should be paid to the underlying conditions necessary for promoting meaningful schooling for girls. This calls for greater coordination across sectors, with the roles of coordinating bodies and mechanisms clearly set out in education policy.

Third, the definition of indicators needs to become part of the process of 'expanding capabilities'. The development of indicators for assessing progress is a critical aspect of development planning, but it attracts insufficient attention. Policymakers are overwhelmingly preoccupied with statistically measurable outcomes. While statistical measures are important, they limit the ability to ask rigorous questions about the outcomes of investment in education for individuals and societies. Indicators provide a window into the vision underlying policy and implementation, and in education today they reveal a lack of interest in analysing the meaning and purpose of education for diverse groups. Attention to the development of qualitative, sensitive indicators is required if education is to move towards greater gender equality and the empowerment of women.

Many of the factors that give rise to childhood poverty and educational deprivation are reproduced through intergenerational transfers of deprivation. Educated parents are more likely to invest in their children's education; in particular, educated mothers are more likely to ensure that their daughters attend school. Even when mothers are uneducated, aspirations for a better life for their daughters are likely to motivate them to want them to go to school. However, mothers are often lone voices, and they need support and resources if they are to have an effective say in household decision-making. Investing in the empowerment of adult women complements strategies to support the schooling of their daughters.

Investment in the following areas is also likely to have a big impact on sustaining the demand for girls' schooling:

- Reproductive health awareness and facilities for young girls to enable them to enjoy good health and a delayed age of pregnancy;

- Working with communities to raise awareness about the importance of female education in general, through implementing legal rights and creating forums for women to collectively address commonly experienced injustices;

- Early childhood care and education (ECCE) programmes and crèche facilities to free young girls from the responsibility of looking after their siblings;

- Proactive public action to promote female schooling through incentives that are well resourced and effectively targeted.

The evidence suggests that successful approaches to improving girls' attendance at school and completion of courses are multisectoral, integrated and cross-cutting. The limitations of sectoral policies become immediately apparent when efforts are made to scale up innovation. As has been argued consistently, multiple strategies require simultaneous attention. Many governments have focused on access to education as a first step. However, it is important at the same time to provide cross-sectoral support to learners and their families, and also to improve the quality and management of schools. The overall management structure of schools needs to be clarified; in many countries, schools are not given the central position that they deserve. They are treated as the outposts of the education system, rather than as its hub or centre. Investing in school governance, and creating relationships of accountability between policy-makers, community members, learners and their guardians, and school management are important reforms that can strengthen local involvement in education in a proactive policy environment.

Despite the fact that education offers a strategic entry point for the promotion of gender equality, national and international approaches still focus on access to schooling, and are weak in their analytical grasp of the complexity of gender issues in education. Thus aid instruments, which are often central to the resourcing and management of education, are as yet failing to meet the challenge of promoting gender equality.

This handbook concludes that there is a need to move beyond expecting national and international bureaucracies to give a lead on this front. Clearly, more complex societal understandings of gender inequality are not easily amenable to bureaucratic modes of planning and implementation that require numerical quantification and clearly deliverable targets. Without partnerships with actors who represent diverse societal processes located in many different places, these disjunctures are likely to remain. Therefore, policy-making processes need to be made more transparent and inclusive at all levels to ensure both that resources are allocated to meet priority gaps and needs, and that diverse voices are heard in the promotion of social equality. Policy-making institutions need to institutionalise such partnerships, which can also contribute to holding public institutions accountable. Where public policy can play a role is in developing strong frameworks of commitment to gender equality and monitoring progress towards these in a systematic and rigorous way.

The structure of this handbook is as follows. Chapter 1 discusses the rationales that have informed policy development in girls' education. Chapter 2 explores new discursive ways of thinking about gender issues in education, and moving towards intrinsic rationales and rights-based frameworks. Chapter 3 focuses on the gendered ideologies underpinning the demand for education in different settings, and Chapter 4 explores gender issues in supply-side measures for achieving universal education. Chapter 5 summarises innovative policies and programmes that have the potential to transform gender inequalities in education access and participation. Chapter 6 maps the key issues in mainstreaming gender within education systems; assesses gender issues in the construction of new aid modalities; and identifies the scope for greater gender mainstreaming in the education sector.

1. Gender, Education and Development

Investing in education is one of the fundamental ways in which nation states and their citizens can work together to achieve long-term development goals and improve both social and economic standards of living. This is borne out by numerous research studies which indicate that high levels of education and development are positively correlated (Herz and Sperling, 2004).

The education of women in particular provides the key to securing intergenerational transfers of knowledge, and long-term gender equality and social change. Globally, development policies have begun to heed this message. Gender equity in access to education now occupies a central place in the global policy discourse on human and social development. Gains made in female education as a result of global advocacy and donor pressure have been significant in some cases; however, in others they are fragile and vulnerable to changes in economic and social environments, and girls and women still struggle to catch up with boys and men in their enrolment rates and achievements. There has been progress, particularly in primary education; but in the secondary and tertiary sectors there are still huge gaps, especially in the countries of South Asia and sub-Saharan Africa. Thus the 'gender gap' persists, despite a well-developed and accepted body of scholarship on the factors that constrain female educational achievement relative to that of men, and despite the prediction of high rates of return on state and household investment in education, especially at primary level.

An integral component of the challenge of achieving universal elementary education (UEE) is how to address the persistent exclusion of diverse groups from the right to and benefits of education. A significant proportion of girls are excluded from schools and formal education institutions. Breaking down these barriers – and identifying measures that address the persistent gender gap in some countries – is a significant challenge for social policy development in the decades ahead.

This handbook attempts to analyse the issues and map out the strategies that can help steer policy-makers and practitioners towards achieving goals that are globally valued but as yet unmet.

The focus on gender mainstreaming in education is an attempt to draw attention to the crucial importance of addressing gender-based inequalities in access to and participation in formal schooling, while at the same time emphasising the importance of transforming institutions of policy, planning and delivery to ensure that these inequalities are systematically tackled. Both these issues are complex challenges, requiring political commitment to gender equity and strong leadership, together with honest and rigorous analysis of progress, backed by the right amounts and kinds of human and material resources. This handbook attempts to analyse the issues and map out the strategies that can help steer policy-makers and practitioners towards achieving goals that are globally valued but as yet unmet.

Two points must be clarified at the outset: this handbook uses the terms education and schooling interchangeably, as a reflection of its focus on formal schooling within the overall theme of education. Adult literacy, lifelong learning and other forms of education are not the focus here, although they are critical dimensions of the Education for All agenda. Secondly, although the focus is on gender, which signifies social relations between males and females and is therefore about both men and women, the discussion is mostly about the schooling of girls, as relatively low rates of female enrolment and participation form the predominant pattern of inequality in education worldwide. Where it is relevant, as in some regions and countries where the reverse is true, the ways in which gender inequalities affect boys are also discussed. Otherwise, the handbook proceeds on the implicit assumption, articulated by UNICEF (2003), that any improvements in schooling that positively impact on girls are likely to benefit boys as well.

Achievements and Gaps

Primary education

Data from the annual *Education for All Global Monitoring Reports* published by UNESCO demonstrate the extent to which such changes in direction are required. The gender goal established as part of the EFA consensus aims to achieve parity in primary and secondary enrolments by 2005. Forty-nine out of 149 countries had achieved gender parity in primary and secondary enrolment by 2005. Fifty-five countries that have achieved the primary education goal or are likely to achieve it by 2015 are unlikely to reach the secondary education goal. And the goal is likely to be entirely missed at both levels by 24 countries, a majority of which are concentrated in sub-Saharan Africa and South and West Asia (UNESCO, 2005).

Gender disparities in primary school enrolments overwhelmingly favour boys.

Box 1.1 Out-of-school Children: Gender Dimensions

UNESCO's *Global Monitoring Report on Education for All 2007* presents the following data on gender differentials for out-of-school children.

Worldwide, 57 per cent of all children out of school in 2004 were girls, down from 59 per cent in 1999. While 117 girls were not in school for every 100 boys, there were regional variations. The ratio of girls to boys who did not attend school was higher in the Arab states (134 girls to every 100 boys) and in South and West Asia (129). Individual countries showed much higher proportions than the global average, for example Yemen (184), Iraq (176) and India (136). The converse was the case in Latin America and the Caribbean, where there were 96 girls out of school for every 100 boys.

The report also notes that *'on average a child whose mother has no education is twice as likely to be out of school as a child whose mother has some education'.*

Gender disparities in primary school enrolments overwhelmingly favour boys. There are some countries where they favour girls – mainly in Latin America, the Caribbean and Europe – but these disparities are usually small and almost all should be eliminated by 2015. Enrolment data are, however, insufficient indicators of the true picture, as in most countries they capture data that are not net of age. Thus the data do not adequately reflect whether the right proportion of children by age and school year are in school.

Repetition rates result in great inefficiencies in provision and also affect the chances of children achieving adequate levels of learning.

Repetition and completion

Promoting access to school is only one, albeit an important, hurdle for countries to cross. Repetition rates result in great inefficiencies in provision and also affect the chances of children achieving adequate levels of learning. The *Global Monitoring Report 2007* (UNESCO, 2007) reported that boys repeat marginally more than girls and that girls tend to stay in school longer than boys, the notable exception being sub-Saharan Africa, where the reverse is the case. In Latin America and the Caribbean, boys are more likely to fail to complete school than girls. In industrialised countries, policies of automatic promotion mean that pupils do not repeat a year's schooling. The highest rates of repetition are found to be in Grade 1, particularly in East Asia and the Pacific, and South and West Asia.

Low transitions between levels of education

As the *Global Monitoring Report 2007* reports, there are wide variations in the proportion of children who move from the last year of primary schooling to the first year of secondary school (the 'transition rate'). Transition rates are over 90 per cent in the developed countries. Low rates are found in some developing countries, sometimes below 70 per cent and as low as 20 per cent in Tanzania. Most regions have considerable intra-regional differences, with significant differences between the highest and lowest country rates.

At secondary level, as many countries have disparities in favour of girls as of boys. Where overall enrolment ratios are low, girls are likely to be at a disadvantage, while disparities at the expense of boys occur in developed countries and several Latin American and Caribbean countries. The higher up the system, the lower girls' participation – with smaller gender gaps in lower than in upper secondary schooling.

Transition rates tend to be more equally balanced in terms of gender than primary school enrolment rates, a point that needs to be understood in the context of overall lower enrolment rates. In many instances these balanced gender ratios reflect the distribution of class privilege, with girls from better-off households more likely to make the transition than boys from poorer households in the same society.

However, once pupils have enrolled in school, gender differences surface in interesting ways. Boys tend to repeat grades more frequently than girls, except in regions where girls outnumber boys in schools (sub-Saharan Africa), and where girls who gain access to secondary schooling have not been adequately equipped to cope with it. Thus both the quantity and quality of primary schooling has a significant impact on girls' performance in school.

Vocational and tertiary education

Data on vocational and other forms of post-secondary non-tertiary education are hard to find, as these services are provided by diverse ministries and other non-governmental actors. Vocational education enrolment is generally high in industrialised countries and fairly low in developing countries. International data are not systematic enough to provide cross-country comparisons, though the data show that women's enrolment in vocational education in developing countries is generally less than half the total in South Asia and sub-Saharan Africa, and greatest in Latin America, the Caribbean and Europe. Where there is parity, questions need to be asked about coverage – post-secondary non-tertiary education is only found in about 40 per cent of all developing countries, according to the *Global Monitoring Report 2003/4* (UNESCO, 2003).

Globally, tertiary education enrolments have risen steadily, with about three-quarters of the growth taking place in developing countries. Progress towards gender parity has to be assessed against the overall levels of participation. These levels vary by region. However, as the *Global Monitoring Report 2003/4* notes, despite greater parity, female participation in higher education is lower in theory-based programmes than in practically-oriented programmes and diminishes even further in advanced research programmes. Within this global pattern there are, of course, variations.

Intersections of exclusion

Global and national aggregate statistics mask variations within countries and obscure the extent to which national policies need to be sensitive to intra-group and intra-regional inequal-

Tertiary education enrolments have risen steadily globally, with about three-quarters of the growth taking place in developing countries.

Eighty-two per cent of out-of-school children in a statistical review of 80 countries lived in rural areas

ities. Many countries that have yet to meet the EFA goals have significant inequalities between social groups, as well as between geographical areas. Eighty-two per cent of out-of-school children in a statistical review of 80 countries lived in rural areas (UIS, 2005). Inaccessible areas, economically and socially underdeveloped because of their terrain or because they are inhabited by social minorities, may be neglected and contain significant numbers of out-of-school children. These differences are not reported for most countries and hence require far greater attention.

> ### Box 1.2 Intersecting Inequalities: Gender and Other Forms of Disadvantage in Asia
>
> All regions of the world have rich mosaics of social diversity, which often give rise to patterns of inequality based on historical developments in the spread of political power and social authority, and uneven regional development. The Asia region has some of the most internally differentiated societies and hence the most marked inequalities, which are evident in educational outcomes, as the following examples show.
>
> In Nepal, caste-based and indigenous group-based inequality in literacy and primary education is particularly pronounced, and is exacerbated by regional variations. The national average literacy rate among Dalits aged 6 years and over is only 23 per cent (12 per cent for women and 33 per cent for men); only 30 per cent of Dalit children go to school. Dalit girls' enrolment is only 42 per cent, indicating a 5 per cent higher gender gap than the national net enrolment ratio (NER) gender gap. Similarly, there is a differential between the indigenous community with the highest literacy rate (Thakali, 79.9 per cent) and that with the lowest (Chepang, 36 per cent). The low literacy rate of these groups has been attributed to the fact that Nepali, the language used for determining literacy, is their second language.
>
> In Bangladesh, poverty is one of the foremost barriers hindering the country from attaining its EFA goals.

Children, especially girls from particularly disadvantaged groups such as the ultra poor, tribal populations, children with disabilities (CWD), and children living in disaster prone areas and urban slums, are unable to attend school. The majority of these children are compelled to work for wages. Moreover, a lack of physical facilities and difficult terrain in remote areas create serious barriers hindering children from attending school.

China's impressive performance in education conceals the disparity in educational attainment among China's estimated 1.185 billion inhabitants. While the goal of nine-year compulsory education has already been achieved in most large cities and coastal areas, many poor and remote areas have not even reached six years of universal primary education. The education system in these areas suffers from insufficient, dilapidated or dangerous classrooms and schools; high numbers of unqualified teachers; poor teaching materials; high drop-out and repetition rates; unsatisfactory management; and difficult access. Many of China's poor and remote areas are inhabited by minority nationalities. Mainly for historical, geographical and cultural reasons, the economic and education levels in many minority areas are lower than the national average.

Gardener and Subrahmanian, 2005

That girls tend to be particularly disadvantaged across all social groups has two implications for policy making. First, the fact that all social groups, whether excluded or not, display gender inequalities, tells us something about the universal nature of gender inequality. Second, the way in which these inequalities are particularly entrenched for girls from groups disadvantaged by geography or social affiliation such as caste, religion or ethnicity suggests that gender intersects with other forms of identity and affiliation to produce differentiated outcomes. These intersections require attention, as they suggest that in addition to cross-cutting gender strategies, particular approaches may need to take into account the overall inequalities experienced by particular groups.

... levels of education among a given population are highly correlated with levels of economic development.

Why Paying Attention to Gender and Education is Important

The rise of interest and belief in the policy returns to investment in education, particularly for girls, is linked to the rise of human capital theory (HCT) in the 1960s. Much of the theoretical debate about the role of education in development and economic growth focused, in that period and subsequently, on whether education could be considered economically productive. The appeal of the argument that views education as an important investment in productivity lies in the simultaneous emphasis on the importance of, and returns to, investment in education for both individuals and states/societies. Education, like health, is seen as a long-term investment, where individuals sacrifice short-term enjoyment for long-term pecuniary and non-pecuniary benefits (Blaug, 1987).

Private returns on investment in education

Human capital theory emphasised the private returns on investment in education by governments, drawing on evidence that levels of education among a given population are highly correlated with levels of economic development. HCT asserts that education creates skills which facilitate higher levels of productivity among those who possess them in comparison with those who do not. The costs of education are thus offset by the associated benefits, a relationship that works both for states and for households as a rationale for investing in education.

Drawing on different proxies for measuring this relationship, human capital theorists provide evidence of positive correlation between wages and salaries and level of education, and empirically demonstrate that higher wages are associated with higher levels of education. A related assumption is made that higher levels of education correlate with higher levels of productivity, thus resulting in the payment of higher wages. Education levels therefore become a useful proxy for employers to assess the potential productivity of their employees. The returns to education were seen to increase through much of the working life of an educated employee as compared with the earnings profile of the less educated, which tends to be flatter over the course of their working lives. This empirically obtained fact was assumed to point to the greater capacity of educated employees to learn on the job and continue to improve their productivity (Oxaal, 1997).

The debate on the value of drawing on HCT has been critical, and positions have been taken on both the flaws in the normative positions that HCT gives rise to, particularly about education itself, as well as on the methodological limitations of such analytical tools. The assumptions about the relationship between education, productivity and income have long been questioned, particularly in terms of the lack of engagement with the social construction of these relationships, and the ways in which labour markets are mediated by social processes of differentiation and recognition. For example, education or schooling itself is argued to be used as a proxy for productivity, functioning more as a device for screening a large pool of available labour, and as a socialisation process for inculcating what are considered to be desired attributes by employers, rather than in terms of the development of particular cognitive skills.

Questions about the direction in which causality works in the debate on the impacts of education on economic development continue to be asked, together with questions about whether private returns to male and female education can be the same, given that labour market discrimination results in inequality in the occupational earnings for women relative to men at given ages and levels of education. Private rates of return (to the household) for female education are, therefore, considered to be less for a number of reasons However, it is argued that public rates of return (to society), which measure externalities such as effects on fertility and child health, are higher for female education than for male (Oxaal, 1997).

... public rates of return (to society), which measure externalities such as effects on fertility and child health, are higher for female education than for male.

Public and social returns

Far more persuasive in terms of its impact on promoting female education as a policy priority for governments and development agencies is a set of arguments detailing the benefits of female education for social development. The shift from focusing on individual and private economic returns to benefits for society as a whole has had a dynamic impact on the attention paid to female education, relative to other kinds of gender equity investments. In 1993, the World Bank published an influential book arguing the case for viewing education for girls as both an economic and social issue. It argued that 'once all the benefits are recognised, investment in the education of girls may well be the highest-return investment available in the developing world' (King and Hill, 1993: v). These benefits included substantial health gains for women and their families, accelerated fertility decline through changes in marriage practices and awareness levels, in addition to the economic benefits discussed above. King and Hill made a strong argument for the case that educating girls was the best way of breaking vicious cycles of poverty and deprivation, leading to improved child mortality rates and more educated children. The case for the intergenerational benefits of educating females was strongly articulated and was subsequently supported by numerous other research studies (see, for example, UN Millennium Project, 2005).

Herz and Sperling (2004) provide a succinct summary of the benefits of girls' education, drawing on a substantial body of research. More education for girls is associated in diverse settings with:

- **Income growth:** for both individuals and nations – it has been argued that returns to secondary education, in particular, are higher for women than for men.

- **Faster economic growth:** again, female secondary education is shown to boost economic growth.

- **More productive farming:** with associated impacts on child nutrition.

- **Smaller families:** fertility decline correlates most strongly with female schooling.

- **Healthier families:** greater levels of immunisation of children, reduced infant mortality and better child survival.

- **Educated children:** educated mothers, in particular, invest more in their children's, particularly daughters', education.

- **Lower chances of contracting HIV/AIDS:** more highly educated girls and women are found to be better equipped to negotiate safer sex; young educated men are also more likely to be aware of and use condoms as a method of HIV prevention. Again, this finding is linked more strongly with secondary schooling completion for girls (Hargreaves and Boler, 2006).

- **Greater empowerment for women:** improving their ability to resist domestic violence; reducing their risk of female genital mutilation; and increasing their political and democratic participation.

This impressive list of the benefits of female schooling draws on studies set in various contexts. Irrespective of an equally rich literature discussing methodological limitations, it has become established as conventional policy wisdom leading to an unprecedented global interest in female schooling, particularly in the last two decades. The relationship between girls' education and fertility decline has, in particular, been frequently revisited by social scientists. Fertility decline, it is argued, accelerates when female education increases, through greater awareness and use of contraceptives and family planning methods, delayed age of marriage and the increased opportunity costs of raising children when economic opportunities are increased. Sathar *et al.* (2003) conclude that:

> … mass schooling is an important determinant of fertility change, particularly when girls are included. It would appear that fertility change will be much more difficult and will come much more slowly when girls are left behind.

It has been argued that the interlinkages between female education and a range of well-being indicators operate through numerous pathways. When marital age is delayed on account of continued schooling, the age of first pregnancy is delayed, resulting in improvements in maternal weight and consequent benefits for child survival. In countries where child marriages (below the age of 18) are common, girls tend to marry earlier than boys. Early pregnancies are also common in such contexts, with almost 10 per cent of all babies born worldwide being born to girls aged 15–19 years of age. Pregnancy-related deaths are the leading cause of mortality for 15–19-year-old girls worldwide. Delaying the age of marriage has important consequences for maternal health and mortality, as well as for child mortality and survival.

Fertility decline … accelerates when female education increases, through greater awareness and use of contraceptives and family planning methods, delayed age of marriage and the increased opportunity costs of raising children …

... there remain significant challenges to achieving gender parity and gender equality in education ...

In particular, the effect of education on women's ability to act independently in their own interests and those of their families and children has been much celebrated (Herz and Sperling, 2004). Schooling is seen as a way of enhancing the status of women in the eyes of their communities; it also increases their 'agency' and gives them confidence to take actions that 'transform society itself' (ibid.: 35). The autonomy-creating effects of schooling are particularly discussed in the literature on the impact of schooling on fertility, and are argued to be a critical explanatory variable for the impact of greater levels of schooling on women's ability to control their fertility. The cause-effect relationship hypothesised between female education and fertility includes the following assumptions:

> *... educated women typically want fewer children than uneducated women ... Among other reasons, this may be because education lowers the preference for male offspring. Education also promotes the agency of women in reducing child mortality (resulting in lower infant and child mortality among educated women), and in improving reproductive health (by contributing to greater awareness and use of contraception among educated women) ... Educated women are thus able to plan and achieve smaller families.* (Murthi, 2002: 1771)

Unpacking 'returns'

Yet, despite this body of evidence, there remain significant challenges to achieving gender parity and gender equality in education, both goals emphasised as globally valued through international dialogues, conference agreements and compacts. It is evident that despite the benefits that states and households stand to gain from investing in female education, there is a disjuncture with household-level demand for universal elementary education for girls. Many social and economic costs continue to undermine the rationale for households to invest fully and equitably in female schooling. The reasons for this 'disconnect' are varied; they are presented below in summary, highlighting the conceptual and methodological limitations of the definition and measurement of 'returns' and the over-simplification of the analysis of the pathways between causes and effects.

1 Thresholds matter

In the discussion of returns to female education, it is also important to take into account the number of years of schooling required to generate benefits. For instance, infant mortality appears to improve with each additional year of female education, while fertility rates appear to require a higher threshold of investment in female education, although there are geographical variations in the latter finding. The spread of secondary and tertiary education is critical for its empowering and redistribution effects, which are especially significant for girls and women in developing societies. Contesting the widely held belief that the highest returns to female education are in the primary sector, Malhotra, Pande and Grown (2003) argue that often it is post-basic education, that is, secondary or higher levels of schooling, that generate greater gender equity. They find that

> ... the frequent U shaped relationship between education and employment indicates that a little bit of education actually is not a meaningful human capital investment in many developing country settings. Gender inequality in wages also seems to be reduced at higher but not lower levels of education. Similarly, several of the studies on health care indicate substantially stronger effects of secondary schooling. The studies on decision-making and gender differentials in child mortality also indicate that it is sometimes only secondary education that has beneficial impact of empowering women or reducing gender inequality.

Investing in female secondary schooling needs to become the policy focus, recognising that some of the most enduring constraints to female schooling originate in the post-puberty years of a young girl's life.

2 Pathways cannot be reduced to simple correlations

Jeffery and Jeffery (1998) argue that pathways between interlinked aspects of human well-being cannot simply be unravelled, as human life is socially organised, and questions of power and context are crucial in determining outcomes. Calculating individual returns to female investment thus defies simple conclusions, as individual decisions are not made independently of wider social norms and influences. A case in point relates to

The spread of secondary and tertiary education is critical for its empowering and redistribution effects ...

Calculating individual returns to female investment thus defies simple conclusions, as individual decisions are not made independently of wider social norms and influences.

decisions about fertility control. Drawing on research in India, Jeffery and Jeffery argue that overall levels of education matter more in predicting lower fertility for all women. That is, where general levels of schooling are high, the contrasts in reproductive behaviour between schooled and unschooled women appear to be far less than in areas where the general levels of education are low. They argue that it is important to focus on understanding the wider economic rationales that may either drive both fertility decline and female education, or drive the former without affecting the latter.

Education alone seldom provides sufficient explanation of changes in child well-being – there are a number of proximate determinants that influence outcomes such as fertility decline, including husband's schooling, regional and caste cultures, female employment and household income. These proximate determinants also exert an influence on the decision to educate females in the first place. For example, McNay (2003) argues that Zimbabwe, one of the demographically advanced countries of sub-Saharan Africa, has achieved demographic transition without expanding women's opportunities in the economic, social and political sphere. Indeed, she suggests that poverty may be driving households to control their fertility. This indicates that fertility decline could take place without investment in female education. On the other hand, gains in female education can be realised without any impact on fertility rates. Fuller and Liang (1999: 184) note that in countries like Botswana or Kenya:

> … *economic commercialisation unfolds, modern rules emerge, female enrollment rises, but fertility behaviour changes only slightly.*

These pathways operate in different ways in different societies, with economic growth and demographic transition driving changes in household investment in health and education in some cases (Kabeer, 2003). In others, proactive policy measures have driven change in social development, without commensurate improvements in per capita income. In yet others, despite economic growth and policy measures, gender inequalities in education persist, as in South Asia, where demographic transition has reduced family size with no automatic effect on gender disparities in education.

While education is clearly an important influence on women's ability to gain access to waged employment, it is not the only means through which women's agency can be enhanced or improvements in well-being achieved. For instance, Drèze and Sen (1995) argue that *both* female education (and literacy) *and* female labour force participation are correlated with positive improvements in female child survival. Citing two Indian states, Kerala and Manipur, they note that female literacy, the prominence of women in influential social and political activities and the tradition of matrilineal inheritance have *all* been important in contributing to the more egalitarian gender relations in these states, which enjoy a much higher level of social development than most other parts of India.

Investments in fertility decline and nutrition may in some cases need to precede changes in female education – in other words, the relationship may work inversely. Reduced fertility can shrink the size of school-age cohorts, possibly freeing up greater public resources for schooling, reduce age-dependency ratios, freeing up household resources for investing in human capital, and/or change social norms guiding opportunities for women by reducing the time they spend on child rearing. This in turn can have greater intergenerational spillover effects, creating more opportunities and incentives for children's and daughters' education in particular (Eloundou-Enyegue, 2004).

Improvements in the nutritional status of women and girls can promote cognitive development of all children – girls and boys. If boys and girls are more equally prepared for school, the gap in enrolment and attainment is more likely to close, as is the gap in their returns to the workforce (ibid.).

Two important points are raised in this discussion. First, the drivers of demographic change are likely to be many: female education is not the only one. Second, even if female schooling is a critical pathway to fertility decline, it cannot be assumed that it is greater female autonomy that is mediating the relationship between the two. The impact of schooling on female autonomy and agency, defined as the capacity to think and act upon interests independently, is extremely hard to establish. This is because gender ideologies, or ways of thinking about the value of women, and the expectations associated with investment in women, often result in an emphasis on

... the drivers of demographic change are likely to be many: female education is not the only one.

Young women are expected to uphold traditions of docility and domesticity, irrespective of the amount of education they receive, and their schooling does little to challenge these ideologies.

women's continued subordinate position within the family, and are rarely challenged by the content of education provided through schooling systems. Jeffery and Jeffery (1998), for instance, explore the meanings of girls' education for families in a highly patriarchal setting, and uncover the dominance of marriage as a driver of female educational investment. They find that irrespective of the level of schooling, the importance of reproducing domestic structures of marriage, rather than opening up employment opportunities, is emphasised by parents. Young women are expected to uphold traditions of docility and domesticity, irrespective of the amount of education they receive, and their schooling does little to challenge these ideologies. Jeffery and Jeffery argue, therefore, that it may be erroneous to assume on a global scale that girls' schooling inevitably contributes to greater autonomy and empowerment of women.

3 Enabling conditions are important for the realisation of outcomes

Education's interlinkages with other aspects of human well-being are indisputable, but all of these aspects of well-being operate within a complex terrain of social relationships, structures, norms and opportunities. This means that often the ways in which these inter-relationships work are hard to understand and defy simplification. Further, they are likely to vary across different contexts and settings. Malhotra, Pande and Grown (2003) reviewed numerous studies from across the world on the impact of investment in education on gender equity, covering indicators of women's health and well-being, their position in family and society, economic opportunities and returns, and political participation. They found that the relationship between education and gender equity was positive, negative or inconclusive, reflecting differences across diverse contexts in key variables of level and type of schooling, the characteristics of the labour market and marital status. They concluded that the research reviewed demonstrated consistently favourable impacts of schooling on maternal health and women's freedom of movement. However, in the remaining indicators of economic returns, political participation and position in the family and society, studies demonstrated the importance of a

range of underlying social and economic conditions in determining whether schooling could positively impact on gender
equity. In other words, female schooling, together with other
aspects of gender equity, were all positively correlated with
more egalitarian societies, well-delivered public services and
well-developed markets.

Whether the effects of investment in female education are
positive or negative depends to a great extent on the 'character of gender relations' in operation in a given context (Drèze
and Sen, 1995). Kabeer (2003) notes that

> ... while absolute levels of education across the world closely cor-
> relate with levels of economic development, it is impossible to
> explain observed patterns of gender inequality in education with-
> out some reference to pattern of gender relations prevailing in
> different contexts.

Jeffery and Basu (1996) also point out that the timeframes and
generations across which diverse outcomes are realised are
wide-ranging, especially where school-going children are first-
generation learners, as in the case of much of sub-Saharan
Africa and South Asia. Reviewing some of the demographic
literature, Heward (1999: 6) notes that 'in patriarchal settings,
... it takes several years of schooling to postpone the age of
marriage', which underlines the point that entrenched structural inequalities are unlikely to shift merely with access to
education. The debate on the impact of education on fertility
decline addresses this from one angle, with a significant body
of literature arguing that it is a country's level of development
and the extent of egalitarianism in gender relations that determine the translation of years of schooling into fertility decline
(Jejeebhoy, 1995; Heward, 1999).

If the character of gender relations has such a heavy bearing on well-being indicators such as the female:male ratio, and
child survival, as Drèze and Sen (1995) argue for India, then
clearly interventions that transform existing patterns of inequality should take priority, and no single intervention, be it in
education, health, personal security or legal rights, is likely, on
its own, to have a transformative impact on women's agency.

Whether the effects of investment in female education are positive or negative depends to a great extent on the 'character of gender relations' in operation in a given context.

Investment in female education is inextricably linked with investment in other forms of gender equality and well-being, including employment and income, health, protection from violence and child survival.

Conclusion

These arguments point to the complexity of the underlying relationships and levels of education required to create positive results for female education. The purpose of this discussion is not to deny that benefits can be derived from investing in female education, but to caution against the flawed assumptions that may flow from an oversimplified analysis of the pathways through which these benefits are delivered. The evidence and debates reviewed above point to two interlinked issues that will be critical in the period ahead, when attempts are made to consolidate gains and tackle enduring constraints.

- Investment in female education is inextricably linked with investment in other forms of gender equality and well-being, including employment and income, health, protection from violence and child survival. In some cases, female education drives changes in gender equality and child well-being as a whole: in others, changes in other aspects of gender equality and well-being have a positive impact on female schooling. Thus, evidence of the returns to female education cannot be used to *sequence* investments in gender equality as a whole by prioritising female education to the exclusion of other investments. An integrated comprehensive approach to all interlocking aspects of gender inequality, including education, has a far better chance of accelerating progress on girls' education than a narrow sectoral approach.

- Secondary education coincides with adolescence and is a critical period in most societies, during which gender ideologies regarding girls' and boys' capacities, roles and freedoms are shaped. Adolescence often marks the point at which gender inequalities in education come to the fore, particularly in countries which are just achieving gender parity in primary education. It is not surprising that studies show that secondary schooling is a defining period for determining returns to female schooling, particularly in terms of impacts on gender equality and for pay-offs in relation to women's empowerment. It is equally unsurprising that girls face the toughest battles to continue with schooling during this phase of their lives. Building linkages between primary and secondary schooling, and identifying ways of promoting a seamless transition between primary and secondary schooling are strategies that will yield higher benefits than piecemeal investments in segments of the education system. The long-held view that investment in female primary schooling yields higher returns than investment in other subsectors of education has given rise to a focus on primary education to the exclusion of other sectors in many countries. Bangladesh provides evidence of the wisdom of investing in female secondary schooling, with a much-lauded scholarship scheme. The country's overall performance in human development has increased and gender parity in primary and secondary schooling have been rapidly achieved.

2. Reframing the Education Policy Discourse: Rights, Capabilities and Empowerment

As the previous chapter argued, instrumentalist arguments, that is, arguments for female education based on its strategic value for states and households, have been a critical determinant of the increased attention paid to girls' education in recent decades. However, they have been intensely scrutinised as discursive frames for female education, and concerns have been raised about their limits. A particular concern is that in focusing on female schooling as a means to wider developmental ends, policy-makers may fail to pay attention to the qualitative changes necessary to win women's rights and equality. The fact that gender gaps in access to education persist, despite the wide acceptance of these persuasive arguments, is also a signal that policy prescriptions that do not address underlying power imbalances and inequalities between women and men are unlikely to plug the gap.

Debates about the importance of investing in female education have received considerable research attention; they will continue to do so as long as the relationship between female education and diverse outcomes continues to defy simplification and evade easy policy prescriptions. Chapter 1 made two key points. First, the inconclusive nature of the evidence points to multiple pathways between means and ends and cause and effect in different settings, and therefore policy and programmatic responses need to be localised to a far greater extent than at present. Second, unless attention is paid to the underlying causes of female disadvantage in education and other aspects of well-being, and the interlinkages between all these dimensions are better understood, female schooling is unlikely to deliver the results expected from it in policy approaches and strategies.

Locating girls' education within the broader sets of gender relations that obtain in different contexts requires conceptual

... the EFA goals focus both on gender parity and gender equality in different levels of education, whereas the gender MDG focuses only on reductions in disparities ...

tools that allow for the interplay between schooling and society to be made explicit in policy and programming. This chapter focuses on the different ideas and concepts relevant to the development of gender-equitable policies in education.

Gender Equality in Education: Framing a Substantive Approach

The 1990s represented an important turning point in international education, marked by the Education for All conference held at Jomtien in Thailand in 1990. Commitments and pledges made by governments and the international aid system are widely used to frame the agenda for change in education. The follow-up World Education Conference (WEF) held in Dakar, Senegal in 2000 to review progress marked a second watershed, where pledges were renewed and commitments refined.

While the 1990 Jomtien consensus advocated a universal approach towards the achievement of EFA by 2000 (without disaggregation of targets by gender or disadvantaged groups), the WEF Declaration recognised that the targets had not been reached by 2000 and moved the target year forward to 2015 in line with the Millennium Development Goals. The consensus at WEF expanded the policy goals to include free and compulsory primary education and placed greater emphasis on quality education (Rose and Subrahmanian, 2005).

EFA goals for gender equality in education go beyond the goals and targets set in the MDGs. First, the EFA goals focus both on gender parity and gender equality in different levels of education, whereas the gender MDG focuses only on reductions in disparities, while recognising education as one of the three levers through which the goal of gender equality and empowerment of women can be met. Second, the MDGs focus narrowly only on universal primary completion, whereas the consensus at both Jomtien and Dakar emphasises the importance of education beyond primary schooling. The EFA and MDG goals taken together represent a strong global message on the importance of education for women as well as progress towards gender equality as a whole.

Box 2.1 EFA and MDG Targets

EFA Dakar Goals

1 Expanding and improving comprehensive early childhood care and education, especially for the most vulnerable and disadvantaged children.

2 Ensuring that by 2015 all children, particularly girls, children in difficult circumstances and those belonging to ethnic minorities, have access to and complete *free and compulsory primary education* of good quality.

3 Ensuring that the learning needs of all young people and adults are met through equitable access to appropriate learning and life skills programmes.

4 Achieving a 50 per cent improvement in levels of adult literacy by 2015, especially for women, and equitable access to basic and continuing education for all adults.

5 Eliminating gender disparities in primary and secondary education by 2005, and achieving gender equality in education by 2015, with a focus on ensuring girls' full and equal access to and achievement in basic education of good quality.

6 Improving all aspects of the quality of education and ensuring excellence of all so that recognised and measurable learning outcomes are achieved by all, especially in literacy, numeracy and essential life skills.

MDGs

Goal 2: Achieve UPE
Target 3: Ensure that, by 2015, children everywhere, boys and girls alike, will be able to complete a full course of primary schooling.

Goal 3. Promote gender equality and empower women
Target 4: Eliminate gender disparity in primary and secondary education, preferably by 2005, and in all levels of education no later than 2015.

... for equality to be achieved, we need a definition that recognises that women and men start from different positions of advantage and are constrained in different ways.

Gender parity

Gender parity as an indicator of gender equality reflects a *formal* notion of equality, defined in terms of access to and participation in education. Formal equality can also be understood as equality that is premised on the notion of the 'sameness' of men and women, where the male actor is held to be the norm. This is reflected in the way gender parity is used in measuring EFA progress, where the gender parity index computes the ratio of female-to-male value of a given indicator, with the mean value being 1.

However, gender parity indicators have two limitations. One arises from the understanding that measuring access to and participation in education, while important, is a limited indicator of change in education, as it does not by itself tell us very much about the processes of education. At best, it is a first-order outcome indicator. Second, it is a 'static' measure. A relational understanding of 'gender' requires recognition of the dynamic processes by which gender inequalities are constituted across different arenas of human life. Gender inequalities arise from the unequal power relations between women and men, and hence assessments of gender equality need to capture the relational dimensions of gender inequality.

Gender equality

The measurement of formal equality is normally based on counting numerical 'gaps' between female and male outcomes. However, for equality to be achieved, we need a definition that recognises that women and men start from different positions of advantage and are constrained in different ways. Thus achievement of *substantive equality* requires the recognition of

> *... the ways in which women are different from men, in terms of their biological capacities and in terms of the socially constructed disadvantages women face relative to men.*

> Kabeer, 1999: 37

This depends on two further processes, indicators of which can tell us *how* equality of outcome has been achieved. These processes refer to the *quality of experience* of education, in terms of entering education, participating in it and benefiting from it. For gender equality to be meaningful, mechanisms for ensuring *equality of treatment* as well as *equality of opportunity* for men and women are important. These in turn rest on a commitment to non-discrimination, to ensure the erasure of social norms that construct women and men as unequal in value in terms of their contributions and entitlements, and to ensure that all social actors are committed to eliminating stereotypes and attitudes that reinforce and perpetuate inequalities in the distribution of resources between women and men. Assessing gender equality thus requires an assessment of whether fundamental freedoms and choices are equally available to women and men. This involves focusing on pathways to equality and extending the concern with treatment and opportunity to look at the agency and autonomy exercised by women in enjoying their freedoms.

A move towards *substantive gender equality* thus requires recognition that discrimination arises from a differential valuation of what it is that men and women contribute, giving rise to differential (unequal) investments in women and men, differential (unequal) rewards paid to women and men, and differential (unequal) resources allocated to men and women. Gender refers to the construction of a social category of differentiation based on biological sex, i.e. a process by which biological differences between women and men (in terms of reproductive capacities and some physiological traits related to these capacities) are converted into processes of social differentiation that result in differential valuations of the capacities, skills, abilities, entitlements and rights of women and men. Such differences in value are as apparent in societies in which girls are excluded from education relative to boys because of the low value allocated to their socially constructed role as carers as they are in societies where the relatively higher academic achievement of girls remains unrecognised and undervalued in the wider economy. Thus, even if opportunities for education are made available to women and they make the best use of them, they may still be prevented from benefiting in the way they should because of discrimination operating outside the sphere of education (Subrahmanian, 2005a).

Gender equity

Therefore, in addition to gender parity and gender equality, the concept of gender equity is important, both for operational

Assessing gender equality ... requires an assessment of whether fundamental freedoms and choices are equally available to women and men.

Recognition that women have multiple affiliations and identities alongside their gender implies identifying strategies to suit the needs and interests of different groups of women.

purposes and for measuring the effectiveness of strategies adopted to achieve gender parity and gender equality. Gender equity is defined here as a policy concept which emphasises the redistribution of resources between women and men in a way that addresses gender-based asymmetries in investment and in the capacities of women and men. That is, gender equity measures are those that recognise that in order to promote equality between women and men to, within and through education, special measures may be required to redress prior inequalities that constrain women's access to and utilisation of resources on an equal basis with men. As argued in Chapter 1, however, gender equity does not mean standardised approaches for all women. Recognition that women have multiple affiliations and identities alongside their gender implies identifying strategies to suit the needs and interests of different groups of women.

Widening the Scope of Gender and Education Interventions: Towards a Rights-based Approach

The rights discourse provides a powerful overarching framework for discussing gender equality, particularly as it has been validated through international dialogue on the nature of international cooperation in recent years. In particular, the citation of human rights in education has a basis in international law, which sets out the legal standards that states commit to when they ratify international treaties. These agreements include the Convention on the Rights of the Child (CRC), the Convention on the Elimination of All Forms of Discrimination Against Women (CEDAW) and the International Covenant on Economic, Social and Cultural Rights (ICESCR). States that have committed to relevant international instruments have clear obligations to progressively realise the right to education and gender equality in and through education (Wilson, 2003). Rights are thus framed in terms of states' obligations towards their citizens, obligations for which they can be held accountable.

The evolution of rights-based approaches (RBA) has been traced historically to the evolution of the UN system after World War II and the subsequent framing of global human rights through various conventions and treaties, as well as to the post-Cold War interest in promoting human development.

> ## Box 2.2 Education as a Universal Right and State Obligation
>
> The right to education has been outlined in numerous international human rights treaties. The Universal Declaration of Human Rights (UDHR) obliged states to provide free and compulsory elementary education as early as 1948. Other treaties that emphasised the obligation to provide free and compulsory education include the International Covenant on Economic, Social and Cultural Rights (1966), the Convention on the Rights of the Child (1989), the UNESCO Convention against Discrimination in Education (1960) and the Charter on the Rights and Welfare of the African Child (1990).
>
> In addition, non-discrimination on the basis of sex has been emphasised in several treaties, including the ICESCR, the International Covenant on Civil and Political Rights (ICCPR), the CRC and the Convention on the Elimination of All Forms of Discrimination Against Women (1979). Protection of rural women is also emphasised in CEDAW, together with measures to ensure equal opportunities for girls to scholarships and eliminate gender stereotyping in the curriculum.
>
> The CRC and CEDAW both elaborate on state obligations to ensure holistic and integrated approaches to education, especially in its content. While CEDAW emphasises access to education in relation to family planning and health, the CRC directs governments to use education to develop respect for human rights and fundamental freedoms, draw attention to the nutritional and health status of children, and ensure that school discipline does not violate human dignity.

These historical shifts in turn relate to concerns about bridging the conceptual and operational distinctions drawn and upheld in practice between human rights and international development, and further between civil and political rights concerns related to the former and poverty alleviation and basic needs concerns associated with the latter. Thus the rise of RBA can be seen in terms not only of bringing together the human rights and development agendas, but also of integrating more successfully within them the discursive and operational parallelism between the economic and social aspects of development goals.

In terms of a historical account of the articulation of rights in relation to development, the institutional reform process embarked upon at the United Nations in 1998 was a significant marker of this approach in contemporary times, evident particularly in the process of defining the 'right to development'. Many international agencies have followed suit and the new discourse has been strengthened by the numerous international conferences of the 1990s, where rights were articulated *inter alia* in relation to reproductive health, women, human rights and social development. Other significant markers of this shift include human rights treaties such as the CRC and CEDAW.

> ### Box 2.3 International Conference Declarations on Gender and Education
>
> In addition to international treaties outlining the obligations of states to citizens and the standards that public policies must meet, global development discourse has been enriched by the international declarations made at a series of conferences in the 1990s. These conferences focused on human rights (Vienna, 1993), population and development (Cairo, 1994), women (Beijing ,1995) and Social Development (Copenhagen, 1995). Together, the deliberations and consensus achieved at these meetings elaborated on human rights standards in a range of intersecting arenas. Education and gender equality received significant attention, albeit framed in different ways, drawing attention to the importance of integrated approaches to delivering public goods.
>
> In all these declarations education is seen as a vital means for women to fulfil their potential and gain access to greater social, political and economic opportunities.

In particular, all the conference documents emphasised the importance of eliminating gender-based violence, sexual harassment and abuse, generally and in particular in the education sector. The importance of gender-sensitive and non-discriminatory curriculum content and transaction was also emphasised, as was the importance of teacher training and ensuring equal numbers of male and female teachers. Linkages with reproductive health rights were made and the right of young mothers and pregnant adolescents to continue their schooling was emphasised.

States and multilateral organisations are also obliged by these declarations to mainstream gender awareness and the human rights of women into their policies and activities, ensure adequate financial allocations to realise these rights and develop specific policies and programmes with a gender perspective.

The active mobilisation of national and international civil society actors working towards bottom-up processes of articulating the rights and entitlements of citizens, particularly those disenfranchised from the processes of agenda-setting and deciding on the distribution of resources at national and local levels, has fuelled the spread of this language.

The increasing articulation of rights as central to development leads to an emphasis on the duty of the state to uphold the rights of its citizens. While providing a new framework for assessing the actions of the state and claiming accountability for resource allocation, distribution and provision, the shift from needs to rights as a basis for development policy and planning places the citizen centre stage. This recasting can provide new and powerful normative frames for promoting well-being in a range of arenas. The spaces thus created through the expansion of international discourse about rights in development can be used by national and local rights advocates to name 'ill-doing' and claim redress.

A rights framework has been developed by Wilson (2003) that captures the interlocking dimensions of gender inequalities and their impact on female education. He identifies a threefold

Conventional measures of educational progress ... fail to measure the extent to which education systems are able to respond to diverse populations and remove gender biases in provisions for diverse learners.

rights framework that encompasses the schooling and non-schooling factors that give rise to education disparities: rights *to* education (access and participation); rights *within* education (educational environments, processes, and outcomes) and rights *through* education (meaningful education outcomes). Extended to gender inequalities in education, this approach to elaborating education rights maps three domains within which strategies and indicators of progress can be developed:

- **Rights to education:** demand and supply factors shaping girls' right to go to school;

- **Rights within education:** supply factors that enable schools to respond to the diverse needs and interests of female and male learners within a wider understanding of gender inequalities in society; and

- **Rights through education:** the extent to which education equips young women and men to enjoy equal opportunities leading to equal outcomes beyond education

These rights are indivisible and hence translate into a substantive programme of action that would promote both gender parity and gender equality.

Rethinking indicators: capabilities and empowerment

The debates around the relationship between female education and social well-being as well as women's empowerment reveal the complexity of the social organisation of human life in different settings and question the simplistic construction of the 'one size fits all' approach. They also raise questions about the basis on which education programming and policies can be developed in a way that provides meaningful change in the lives of women and men, girls and boys. Conventional measures of educational progress focus on the extent to which girls are able to access existing systems of provision. They fail to measure the extent to which education systems are able to respond to diverse populations and remove gender biases in provisions for diverse learners. Making education systems accountable to learners requires indicators of both the extent to which learners access, participate and complete education, and the extent to which education systems respond to learners, create conducive learning environments, and motivate and encourage learners to gain as much as they can from their participation.

The shift to a focus on rights thus emphasises the obligations of the state and provider to the citizen and learner. Yet, mediating the relationship between individuals and the state are complex social relationships and people's multiple affiliations to communities of residence, identity and language. As Chapter 1 showed, over-emphasis on the 'returns' of education, either to the individual or to society as a whole, places the focus on either one or the other, when in reality individuals and societies are bound together in complex ways. While it is very relevant to stress the importance of the realisation of the rights of every individual, it is also vital to recognise that socially constructed norms and values can have a significant bearing on every individual's ability to fulfil their rights.

The capabilities approach, developed by Amartya Sen, and extended by Nussbaum (2000) to considerations of women and development, seeks to provide a powerful cross-cultural normative framework for gender justice. The emphasis on a normative framework that cuts across cultures is required in order to put forward some core universal human values that can form the basis of constitutional projects (with implications for development policy and intervention).

The capabilities approach offers important resolutions to some of the issues raised earlier in terms of the limitations of human capital theory. First, the approach shifts the evaluative lens to a focus on an individual woman's capacities and outcomes, asking 'What is she actually able to do and to be?' By valuing each person as an end, it makes the individual woman the subject of concern, over and above the competing affiliations and identities that may relegate her personhood to secondary status. This approach explicitly rejects evaluative approaches that focus on the 'aggregate benefits an initiative has for the whole society or for future generations, without regard to how it affects individuals' (Unterhalter, 2003: 1).

Second, by emphasising the importance of the achievement by individuals of valued 'freedoms', the capabilities approach places an obligation on governments to establish and sustain the conditions for each and every individual, irrespective of gender, caste, race, to achieve valued outcomes (ibid.: 6). In

The capabilities approach ... makes the individual woman the subject of concern, over and above the competing affiliations and identities that may relegate her personhood to secondary status.

particular, this entails not just structuring opportunities for citizens to expand their capabilities, but also allowing spaces for debate and discussion in the process of expanding capabilities that are valued. The role of public policy, therefore, is to facilitate and enable the substantive freedoms and agency of citizens to debate and utilise public spaces for expanding their capabilities.

The capabilities approach shifts thinking about gender and education away from concern with a

> ... predetermined form of education (a resource-based view) and standardised measurement of gender equality, possibly linked to access or achievement, but rather with the nature of education valued by individual women and men and the conditions that allow them to express these views and realise these valued 'beings and doings. Unterhalter (2003)

Women's education, seen through this lens, becomes not just an end, but a means to enjoying substantive freedoms in society, and a critical space in which to debate and discuss what is valued.

Women's empowerment

The capabilities approach provides a powerful normative public policy framework for thinking about the linkage between individual rights and the wider societal value framework within which these rights can be claimed and enjoyed. Yet for women in many societies, issues of power and autonomy continue to constrain their ability to claim their rights and determine their ability to achieve their capabilities. Women's empowerment, within a framework that recognises individual rights or freedoms to achieve their potential, refers to the processes whereby women's capacities to make purposive choices are enhanced and enabled through supportive opportunity structures which encourage these choices and help develop these capacities (Alsop and Heinsohn, 2005). Public policy thus has a critical role in facilitating women's empowerment through creating supportive opportunity structures for women to make choices that are in line with their wishes and interests.

The way in which Kabeer (2001: 18–19) defines empowerment unpacks the central notion of 'power' in terms of the

... ability to make choices: to be disempowered therefore implies to be denied choice. Empowerment thus refers to the expansion in people's ability to make strategic life choices in a context where this ability was previously denied to them.

Empowerment thus has two components: the kinds of *assets* (material or non-material) that an individual has and can use to make purposive choices, and the kinds of *choice* that is made available through the existing structures and contexts within which the individual is engaged (Alsop and Heinsohn, 2005). Both are necessary for capabilities. Relevant questions thus become those of process and context:

- Does the choice exist?

- Does the person make use of the choice?

- What outcome does the exercise of that choice result in?

Kabeer's (1999a; 2001) schema for measuring interlocking dimensions of change that transform women's capabilities provides a useful way of thinking about indicators of change that are sensitive to this complexity.

Choice has three inter-related dimensions:

- Resources or the conditions under which choices are made;

- Agency or 'the ability to define one's goals and act upon them';

- Achievements – or the outcomes of choices.

Such a schema, applied to female schooling, helps to locate education as one resource among many which have the *potential* to transform women's lives. Thus access to this resource fulfils only one condition of empowerment: the other conditions are the extent to which access helps to strengthen women's agency and whether women's agency, in addition to access to the resource, actually leads to beneficial outcomes in terms of women's capabilities.

Table 2.1 maps out some elements of applying an empowerment approach as outlined by Kabeer (2001) to an analysis of rights in education, leading to the development of indicative measures for assessing the 'conditions of choice' in both the demand for and supply of education.

Table 2.1 Measuring Rights and Empowerment in Education

Conditions of choice	Possible indicators	
	Supply-side	Demand-side
Resources: Access to schooling, cost of schooling, quality of infrastructure	• Availability of schools within reasonable distance of all habitations • Supportive measures to enable children to reach school – transport, residential schools, crèches, all-weather roads and bridges • Cost of schooling • Availability of childcare • Sensitivity to mother tongue of learners • Availability of toilets, water • Measures to secure safety of learners as they move between school and home • Compulsory schooling and enforcement of age at marriage laws	• Adequate income, livelihood security to afford schooling for all children, nutrition and health • Ensuring girls reach school safely • Equal distribution of household resources and responsibilities between boys and girls • Awareness of legal restrictions on early marriage and other gender-biased cultural practices
Agency: Content of schooling, curriculum transaction, equitable treatment within the classroom	• Representations of women and men in curricula • Attention paid to gender equality as a topic or theme • Subject choice at higher levels of schooling • Teacher capacity and behaviour relating to gender issues within the classroom and wider society • Encouragement to learners, regardless of sex, to question dominant forms of knowledge and authority	• Parental or guardian involvement and time given to learning of both boys and girls • Parental or guardian support to girls and boys to sit and pass examinations • Regular interactions of parents or guardians with schools and teachers to discuss child's progress, irrespective of sex and and ability • Awareness of child's experiences in school regardless of parental literacy • Equal participation of girls in, science, mathematics
Achievements: the outcomes of choices	• Skilled labour force • Reduced gender gap and creation of a level playing field for women and men • More engaged citizenship of both women and men	• Freedom of choice relating to marriage • Opportunities to take up employment or study further • Capacity to exert voice and contribute to political and

Conclusion

Current levels of female participation in schooling are unprecedented – signalling success in terms of the strategies that have been employed by governments and international, national and local development agencies to facilitate greater female schooling. However, gaps persist and gains are not yet fully sustainable. To take the movement for female education further, new paradigms, approaches and strategies are required. Three main conclusions emerge from the review of shifting paradigms in thinking about female education.

Advocacy for education as a whole is necessary if advocacy for girls' education is to succeed

Investment in programmes for girls' education needs to be matched by overall improvements in education systems, especially in relation to improving the quality of teaching and curriculum transaction. Too often, girls' education is discussed as a distinct set of concerns, and separated from discussion on reforming education systems as a whole. The two are fundamentally linked. Specific measures for improving girls' enrolment and participation will only succeed if the overall policy packages are pro-equity, pro-poor and pro-marginalised groups.

Interlinkages between education and other investments in human well-being are important

This is particularly true for female education, where the interlinkages between health, nutrition, employment opportunities and education are mutually influential and therefore need to be addressed in a joined-up way. The underlying conditions necessary for promoting meaningful schooling for girls require far greater attention. This calls for greater coordination across sectors, with coordination bodies and mechanisms clearly outlined as part of policy in the education sector.

The definition of indicators must become part of the process of 'expanding capabilities'

The development of indicators for assessing progress is a critical activity in development planning, but one that attracts little attention. Policy-makers tend to be overwhelmingly pre-occupied with statistically measurable outcomes. While statistical measures are important, they substantially limit the scope for rigorous questioning of the outcomes of investment in education for individuals and societies. Indicators provide a window into the vision underlying policy and implementation, but in the case of education they point to the lack of analysis of the meaning and purpose of education for diverse groups. New indicators are required if education is to move towards a vision of greater gender equality and empowerment for women.

3. The Gendered Construction of the Demand for Girls' Education

Widening the scope of analysis and intervention in relation to female schooling requires significant conceptual shifts, as well as the development of new capacities among policy-makers and practitioners. A gender-aware approach to equality is based on the recognition that gender inequalities have been historically legitimised by societies in ways that require careful analysis.

The construction of gender inequality across the world has rested on 'naturalising' a range of differences between women and men in order to legitimise differential treatment and inequality of resource distribution. The unequal burdens borne by women and young girls in reproductive activities, including the maintenance of human resources through their unpaid work within the home, provides a powerful example. It is often assumed that women perform these roles voluntarily and as a result of their natural instincts, rather than recognising that the division of labour is socially determined, creating asymmetries between women and men in the distribution of resources and power. 'Naturalising' these differences has over time translated into entrenched social norms that define appropriate behaviours for men and women, becoming widely accepted as a cultural sanction for the unequal treatment of women. These *gender ideologies* in turn inform masculine and feminine identities. Masked as 'culture', these identities and ideologies often become stubbornly defended as traditional and immutable. Further, they are encrypted in institutions that govern daily life, and thus translate into deeper structural inequalities that are unlikely to be removed unless there are clear efforts to change social rules both through proactive policy measures and the creation of new opportunities for women.

The social construction of gender identity, or what it means to be a woman or a man in a given context, is underpinned by prevailing ideas about the roles that are appropriate for men or women and how what is done by women and men is valued,

The interplay of gender with other forms of social identity gives rise to variations in the inequality experienced by different women.

both socially and economically. Most societies observe some gender division of labour within the home, with women taking primary responsibility for caring for the family, while men tend to be associated with work outside the home, often on a paid basis. This division of labour goes some way towards explaining the gender inequalities in human capabilities which can be observed in a number of contexts.

Gender ideologies vary over time and across societies, and gender identities are also influenced by other social identities, including religion. The interplay of gender with other forms of social identity gives rise to variations in the inequality experienced by different groups of women. Thus gender equity measures for women who are positioned differently on account of their race, ethnicity, economic class, caste or religion need to take into account both the various constraints on, and opportunities for, their full participation in development.

The 'geography' of gender inequality also shows differences between countries and regions in the levels of freedom granted to women. Kabeer (2003) notes that the extent to which women have the freedom to take up paid work outside the home is an indicator of the freedoms granted to women in general, with the most marked gender inequalities found in societies in which women are confined to the home and denied opportunities for paid work. This, she argues, is because restricting women to the home is associated with other forms of unequal resource distribution, including patrilineal principles of inheritance, patriarchal structures of authority within the home and community, and patrilocal systems of marriage where women leave their natal homes and maintain little contact with them after marriage. Women's economic and social dependence on their husbands is often near-complete in such societies. Kabeer also notes that these societies are also characterised by marked son-preference, leading to systematic discrimination against females from birth, reflected in the adverse sex ratios found in most parts of South Asia (with notable exceptions such as Sri Lanka), North Africa, South Korea, Taiwan and China).

In other societies, while restrictions placed on women may not be as extreme as the forms of patriarchy described above, women's responsibilities for domestic work and childcare constrain their full participation in the economy, reinforcing the view that education for women is of secondary importance. This is particularly so in societies where education is not compulsory or where compulsion is not enforced,

Gender inequalities also play out across different areas of life and across the institutions that govern everyday lives. They are constructed or challenged in the everyday life of the family or household, the labour market and the communities (geographical, socio-cultural and political) to which people belong, as well as in the organisations of the state – bureaucracies, the judiciary, political decision-making bodies and public services. These institutions reproduce gender inequalities in their rules and norms, as well as their practices (Kabeer and Subrahmanian, 1999), and reinforce the reproduction of these gender identities over time and space. However, changes in the rules, norms and practices of any one of these institutions can have powerful implications for change in the others – for example, proactive policy measures can provide powerful signals and incentives to households to change discriminatory behaviours; and households which choose to promote their daughters' schooling may generate change by demanding better service delivery for girls and act as role models for other members of their community.

Proactive policy measures for gender equality include paying attention to women's unpaid responsibilities, particularly in relation to human reproduction, which remain undervalued and hence uncompensated, and are a barrier to women's full and equal participation in education. Recognition of these barriers, however, must include attention to other obstacles that arise as a consequence of the internalisation of women's self-perception (often reinforced by society) of their lesser abilities or value. Thus gender equity measures must be both gender-aware and must transform gender relations in the ways in which they operate within the possibilities offered by the environment in question.

Gender Inequalities and Education

Decision-making about the distribution of resources among members of the household is shaped by socially constructed beliefs about what is necessary or appropriate for different genders and different age groups. Decision-making is often a

Proactive policy measures for gender equality include paying attention to women's unpaid responsibilities, particularly in the arena of human reproduction, which remain undervalued and ... are a barrier to women's full and equal participation in education.

process of bargaining, with final outcomes reflecting differences in the degree of bargaining power exercised by different household members (Kabeer, 1994). Bargaining power can be derived from the economic resources that individual members can 'fall back on' on in the absence of consensus or cooperation, such as earnings or inheritance. However, bargaining power can also derive from ideas and perceptions about the different contributions of different household members and the differential valuation of these contributions. These perceptions may be shared by women and men, to the extent that women have a low sense of self-worth, leading them to accept without challenge an unequal distribution of resources. This acceptance may also be strongly influenced by the wider social environment which determines the level of acceptance for a more egalitarian distribution of resources within the family, through the legal framework and redistributional policies.

Box 3.1 The Intergenerational Dimensions of Education Deprivation

The 'vicious' cycle of gender inequalities in education requires proactive action to disrupt what have become 'normalised', and hence accepted, patterns of gender inequalities. The intergenerational cycle of deprivation is well recognised in relation to the patterns of negative outcomes for children associated with household poverty and social exclusion. Intergenerational transmission of poverty shapes the socio-economic opportunities of children and young people. In particular, there is a strong correlation between parental, and especially maternal, education and children's schooling, reported from different countries. Recently, the focus on intergenerationally transmitted poverty has been revived in work on chronic poverty, where 'poverty that spans generations' is seen as 'both a characteristic and cause of chronic poverty' (Moore, 2001: 4).

The lack of longitudinal data in developing countries has meant that this approach to understanding childhood and adult poverty is under-studied or under-utilised. While some studies measure the impact of parental education on outcomes for children (such as nutrition, health access and education), there are few that assess the processes through which these outcomes are shaped.

Central to the concept of intergenerationally transmitted poverty is a focus on relationships, relevant for the 'transfer of resources between generations' (McGregor *et al.*, 1999, cited in Moore, 2001: 7). These relationships are based on implicit 'contracts' – or normative understandings of the rights and obligations that underpin them. An important set of mediating factors determines the relationship between carers and dependents. One is the gender of the carer and the dependent; another is the motivation of the carer and, where there are two people (as in a two-parent family), the distribution of power underpinning the relationship between the carers and the spread of the burden of care. While the idea of inter-generationally transmitted poverty as being based purely on the altruistic intentions of the household head has been successfully challenged (Folbre, 1994; Kabeer, 1994; Kabeer, 2000), intergenerational transfers do rely to some extent on altruistic motivation, particularly where relationships are based on 'close genetic links' (Collard, 1999: 7). However, Collard notes that altruism alone is unlikely to sustain the generational bargain, as there are likely to be trade-offs implicit in resource-constrained contexts. Strategic 'self-interest' may oprate alongside altruism to shape decisions on generational transfers – and different forms of transfer may have different underlying motivations.

The idea of 'trade-offs' is central to understanding both intergenerational and intra-household strategies. The acceptance that the household is a site for resource allocation where relations are determined as much by bonds of affection as by unequal entitlements determined by age and gender (Kabeer, 1997) makes intergenerational transfers complex and likely to be subject to idiosyncratic change (Collard, 1999).

... even if opportunities are presented to women, the nature of their reproductive responsibilities or burdens, which are often time-intensive and home-based, may prevent them from gaining equal access to the opportunities that may in theory be available to them.

Families are critical sites for decisions about life in general and schooling in particular, and it is often parents who make trade-offs between schooling for their children and their livelihoods or position within the community. The reproduction of social roles and the ideologies that underpin them conveys particular sets of values and choices to future generations; this happens implicitly via the gender roles that members of the household play, and explicitly as a consequence of the gender frameworks within which children of each sex are brought up. Households allocate time for different activities among their members and they also allocate resources – for consumption, savings and investment, including those associated with the formation of human capital. These allocations are influenced by the broad social and institutional framework of custom and opportunity in which households are located. Nevertheless, changing the factors that affect household constraints, opportunities and incentives is a critically important means of influencing their decision-making.

Prevailing norms about what women and men do, and how their activities and roles are to be valued, determine their educational opportunities. Thus households may discriminate, as they often do, against girls in favour of boys in access to education. These are clearly relative phenomena, as boys are also likely to be excluded from school in some contexts of poverty or conflict, but where children are sent to school, boys are often advantaged over girls. This means that even if opportunities are presented to women, the nature of their reproductive responsibilities or burdens, which are often time-intensive and home-based, may prevent them from gaining equal access to the opportunities that may in theory be available to them. Thus education may be available to girls and boys, but constraints arising from the nature of the work that girls do may impede their ability to participate in schooling. There are many examples of girls being unable to attend school because their work within the home is far more time-intensive than work undertaken by boys in return for wages: thus girls' work is often incompatible with schooling, whereas boys' work is more likely to be compatible.

Even where women are able to negotiate their burdens so that they can take up opportunities, gender inequalities are often institutionalised in the norms, processes and structures of interventions and institutions, and present barriers to equitable outcomes. Teachers' attitudes, the nature of the curriculum, harassment, concerns about safety and the quality of the infrastructure may all push girls out of school.

Finally, the pervasiveness of social norms that curtail freedoms for women, which are based on undervaluation or devaluation of what they do, can lead women themselves to internalise negative self-perceptions and doubt their own abilities. Thus women often exclude themselves from opportunities that are on offer, and active encouragement may be necessary to support them in challenging internalised social norms that place informal barriers on their participation. The importance of focusing on how the content and processes of education enable women to challenge negative evaluations of their own worth by strengthening their ability to advocate on their own behalf must be part of any consideration of progress towards gender equality in education. Opportunities outside and beyond education can also play a significant role in shaping girls' and boys' aspirations, by challenging or reinforcing stereotypes about typical feminine and masculine attributes, traits and abilities. Focusing on the aspirations that girls and boys articulate can tell us something important about how opportunities and rewards are perceived to be gender-differentiated by young people, with the result that gender inequalities are perpetuated rather than challenged as they leave educational institutions and enter adulthood.

... women often exclude themselves from opportunities that are on offer, and active encouragement may be necessary to support them in challenging internalised social norms that place informal barriers on their participation.

Structural Determinants of Female Disadvantage in Education

The factors which determine the relative disadvantage faced by girls in access to and participation in education thus cut across countries, sectors and institutions. To map these constraints we follow an approach suggested by Kabeer (2004) for analysing the social dimensions of inequality. She identifies the reproduction of life (birth, care of family and childcare), the reproduction of labour (physical labour, human capital and human capabilities) and the reproduction of society (ideological and social conditions) as three distinct but fundamentally interlinked domains underpinning everyday human life. The universality of these domains across the world allows for

Control over marriage and sexuality is one of the key factors restricting girls' education.

comparisons in the ways in which gender ideologies, norms and opportunities operate across different societies. Such an approach does not deny the possible impacts of different institutions, economic and labour market structures and the rapid change facilitated by globalisation or the demographic transition on the prospects for female education in various settings.

Below we focus on two aspects that shape household demand for female education: the relation of education to life and to labour. The third dimension, education and the reproduction of society, is addressed in the following chapter, which focuses on the supply of schooling.

Reproduction of life and its relation to education

Marriage and the family are primary institutions in all societies, though they may be structured in different ways, and women's and men's identities remain centrally defined by these institutions. A significant trade-off is perceived to exist between girls' education and their conformity with the social expectation that they should marry and bear children. In societies where education is seen to convey both opportunity and a degree of autonomy and capacity to act as an agent (i.e. to be in a girl's own interests), school attendance may reinforce parental concerns that their daughter may acquire new ideas that may lead her to defy convention and bring dishonour upon her family by rejecting community norms. Control over marriage and sexuality is one of the key factors restricting girls' education. This is confirmed both by qualitative accounts of education in a variety of settings, as well as by evidence from countries such as Iran which have made rapid progress towards gender parity through promoting conservative or 'value-based' education, which has enabled parents to feel more confident about the impact of education on their daughters (Mehran, 2003).

Finding ways to make households value changes in the opportunities and freedoms for daughters is a long-term project with significant implications for education. In the short term, programmes that encourage girls in school and work with families and communities to persuade them of the value of girls' education may help to shift household views and reproductive strategies. Girls themselves are often drivers of change, going to great lengths to attend school. They work hard and often outperform boys if given an equal chance. But for parents, girls' schooling may still represent a risk. Hierarchies of authority within the family may also mean that decision-makers are often tied into more traditional ideas about what is appropriate and may inaccurately represent the aspirations of children.

Opposition to girls' education may arise out of a fear of change and of the impact of girls' education on social relations within the home and community, and social customs particularly around marriage and childbearing. In a study carried out in Ethiopia, some parents mention the concern that after 12 years of schooling their daughters would be unable to perform housework or be unable to find a husband because they would be too old. Parents also sometimes *assume* that they know their daughters' aspirations and say that girls are interested only in marriage. Some views also reflect an awareness of the nature of existing social conditions for girls and women who break traditional norms – some fathers noted that girls face problems when they cannot find a husband or employment opportunities; they will grow older, have to stay with their parents and bring shame upon the family. Their only option will then be to migrate to a town and lead a miserable life working as a house servant or even as a sex worker (Colclough *et al.*, 2003).

In situations where the prospect of female autonomy is considered unstable or risky, marriage is a way of securing a daughter's future. Early marriage emerges as a significant factor impeding girls' progress in many countries. Girls in the age-group 15–19 are significantly more likely to be married than their male peers in several countries (Wilson, 2003; UNESCO, 2003). Marriage of children and adolescents under the age of 18 is very common in some parts of the world, but its prevalence is difficult to assess. Many such marriages are not registered. Small-scale studies show, however, that country data significantly underestimate its prevalence (Save the Children, 2003).

The marriage market may not discourage education, but it may well shape what is considered to be appropriate or adequate education for girls. Jeffery and Jeffery (1998) note that in rural areas of the Indian state of Uttar Pradesh, concerns about finding an appropriate match for their daughters prompts

Early marriage emerges as a significant factor impeding girls' progress in many countries. Girls in the age-group 15–19 are significantly more likely to be married than their male peers in several countries.

45

In many countries, adolescent pregnancy, both within and outside marriage, constitutes a major cause of the discontinuation of girls' schooling.

parents to seek to educate them to the level considered necessary to inculcate the appropriate skills and credentials. The level of education of girls has to be lower than that of prospective husbands, so as to retain asymmetries between the genders in highly patriarchal settings. In different settings, girls may pursue apprenticeships as a way of developing skills and assets that they can bring into marriage. Hashim (2005) notes that in some areas of Ghana girls are expected to bring into marriage articles considered necessary for setting up house, such as pots and basins, as well as skills for income-generating activities, such as tailoring. This leads young women to migrate from home to areas with better vocational education opportunities before marriage to build the required skills and assets, and to secure a better marriage as well as some economic independence and respect.

Social pressures on girls and boys crystallise around the age of puberty and the development of adolescent sexuality. In many countries, adolescent pregnancy, both within and outside marriage, constitutes a major cause of the discontinuation of girls' schooling. Eloundou-Enyegue (2004) finds that pregnancies are the leading cause of girls dropping out of secondary school in three countries – Central African Republic (37%), Mozambique (25.8%) and South Africa (36.1%) – and the second leading cause in a further six countries – Cameroon (22%), Chad (20%), Gabon (29.8%), Kenya (30.8%), Uganda (28%) and Zambia (25.9%). The high cost of education is believed to lead girls to form relationships with older men in return for gifts and money to help them pay for their schooling. Despite re-entry policies aimed at stemming the high drop-out rate in some African countries, such as Malawi and Guinea, the reluctance of both parents and girls to return to school, because they fear ridicule or are afraid that they may become pregnant again, leads to drop-out becoming irreversible.

Sexual maturation is often a framing experience of adolescence and may render girls particularly vulnerable to rituals and practices that further entrench ideologies of domesticity and sexual subservience, or serve to reinforce beliefs about the differences in the sexuality of boys and girls. Rites of passage for boys and girls differ around the world, but in most cases they reflect gendered norms and beliefs about appropriate roles for men and women in adult life. Many cultural practices aim to address the future gender roles of boys and girls and their rites of passage to the adult world, particularly in relation to puberty, marriage and sexuality. These cultural practices often emerge from or reinforce prevailing discriminatory attitudes against particular groups of children, be they girls, disabled young people or those from particular ethnic groups. These cultural practices often change (sometimes for the worse) with ruptures in the social order, such as conflict-induced displacement or migration, increasing poverty or pandemics such as HIV/AIDS. This shows that cultural practices are not immutable, but they are often presented as legitimated by religion or tradition.

Box 3.2 The 'Feminisation' of HIV/AIDS and its Relationship with Schooling for Girls

Over the past 15 years, economic downturns and the HIV/AIDS epidemic have increased the dependency burden placed on working adults by increasing unemployment or by depleting the adult population. (Eloundou-Enyegue, 2004); this has disrupted the intergenerational transfer of assets and resources by creating a large population of orphans.

The 'feminisation' of HIV/AIDS has begun to attract policy attention, particularly in the light of evidence that girls and women are being disproportionately infected by the virus, especially in sub-Saharan Africa. Data show that feminisation of the epidemic is taking place particularly in this region, where women make up 57 per cent of those who are HIV-positive and where an estimated 17 million women were living with HIV at the end of 2003. Unlike other regions, studies suggest that *young women in the region are two to seven times more likely to be infected with HIV than young men* (Hargreaves and Boler, 2006: 9). Reasons for the vulnerability of young women are associated with greater sexual vulnerability and in particular with inability to enforce 'safe sex', especially in relationships with older men (ibid.). Increasing this vulnerability are a range of reproductive health issues, as well as factors relating to women's bodily integrity and

The effects of HIV/AIDS reach far beyond those immediately affected, and can have devastating consequences for families of victims, and especially for women.

safety from sexual violence. As Hargreaves and Boler (2006: 35) argue: *'Girls and women are vulnerable to HIV simply because they do not have enough power to protect themselves from infection. In order not to be infected with HIV, a woman has to have control over who she has sex with, as well as when and how to have sex. The sad reality is that, in too many countries, only men have this power.'*

The effects of HIV/AIDS reach far beyond those immediately affected, and can have devastating consequences for the families of victims, and especially for women. In families affected by AIDS women in particular are often forced to abandon or delay farming activities to care for family members or to engage in wage labour to cover medical expenses or buy food. In addition, gender biases in food distribution can leave women and girls more susceptible to decreased household food availability. A key challenge, therefore, is to implement integrated responses to address HIV/AIDS, food security and gender equality.

Female schooling has the potential to serve as a powerful protective barrier against the spread of HIV/AIDS, but only under certain conditions. These conditions pertain to the quality of schooling, particularly the extent to which the content and processes of learning enable young women to be empowered; to make decisions that are in their interest and not harmful to them; to negotiate sexual encounters with increased awareness of sexual health; and to have a better ability to deal with general health risks and seek appropriate information. A 32-country study found that women with post-primary education are five times more likely than illiterate women to know the facts about HIV/AIDS. For example, literate women are three times less likely than illiterate women to think that a healthy-looking person cannot be HIV-positive and four times less likely to believe that there is no way to avoid AIDS (Vandemoortele and Delmonica, 2000, cited in UN Millennium Project, 2005: 65).

However, where female schooling takes place in environments where little or no attention is paid to the sexual vulnerability of girls at school, or where discriminatory attitudes remain, schooling may intensify vulnerability.

The interplay between conflict and HIV/AIDS is also highlighted by the greater vulnerability to the virus of young people living in conflict situations. Conflict brings with it the use of sexual violence as well as an increase in sex work where livelihoods are destroyed, resulting in destitution. The Democratic Republic of Congo is an example of a country in conflict which has seen a sharp increase in HIV/AIDS.

The conflation of female identity with the responsibility for the burden of care within the family continues to be a fundamental constraint to female schooling. The low valuation of females relative to males in terms of evaluating productivity and returns to the household determines the ways in which resources are invested in girls and women. The implicit belief is that daughters marry away, and that it is sons who care for elderly parents. However, changes in the economy, with greater incentives for women to work, combined with evidence from many societies that daughters are often more likely to care for elderly parents than sons, have started to change this situation and are giving an impetus to female education. Evidence of this comes from South-east Asia, where ideologies of female docility and caring are beginning to change with the opening up of new economic opportunities and subsequent delays in the age of marriage and childbearing. These changes have also created incentives for families to educate their daughters (McNay, 2003).

However, the extent to which these changes represent real choices for women and reflect greater gender equality is debatable. Many young women's educational choices are shaped by considerations of the trade-off between having children and having the means to return to work with a guarantee of childcare and/or better wages to enable them to purchase childcare services. Furthermore, gender ideologies may not break down

... in Taiwan, ... investment in female education increased to just the level that enabled girls to get jobs that then supported greater levels of investment in the education of sons

as easily as these changes suggest. Investment in female education may also result from considerations that are based on underlying gendered norms. For instance, in Taiwan Greenalgh (1985, cited in Baden and Greene, 1994) found that investment in female education increased to just the level that enabled girls to get jobs that supported higher levels of investment in the education of sons, which in turn derived from the view that daughters' income can be more easily used by families to support household expenditure.

Household investment and capital determine school participation in a variety of ways. The health status of children plays a key role in determining their ability to remain in school. Given gender disparities in health, nutrition and health-seeking behaviour which discriminate in favour of boys, in most developing countries boys are healthier than girls, thus facilitating their school attendance. Parental education also has an impact on the education of children, particularly that of mothers' on their daughters' prospects of attending school (Leach *et al.*, 2003a; 2003b), although in many countries the high levels of adult illiteracy, particularly female illiteracy, indicate that many children in school today are first-generation learners. Household size is also an important factor (Rose and Al-Samarrai, 1997). Larger numbers of children in a family can allow for some children to be educated and not others; in most cases girls suffer relative to boys as they are more likely to be expected to perform domestic tasks. Family birth order also plays a critical role, as older children may be withdrawn from school to provide financial support for the education of younger children.

Thus a variety of household factors can intervene to shape the differential participation of girls and boys in schooling, and these variables combine in different contexts to give rise to different patterns. These are gender-intensified disadvantages, where factors pertaining to poverty and livelihoods affect both boys' and girls' participation, but they are felt more by girls because a lower value is placed on their education. However, as is evident from the data on school attendance, there are gender gaps throughout the education system in many countries. This indicates that gender is a consistent variable in parental decision-making and that girls face gender-specific disadvantages arising from the specific construction of femininity that obtains almost universally.

Perceptions of vulnerability range from sexual violence to innuendo and rumour about girls' reputations, which are of concern to parents who seek good marriage prospects for their daughters. The fulfilment of parental responsibility is not expressed merely by investment in children's education, but can be more realistically assessed in terms of framing parental responsibility as the achievement of what is in the 'best interests' of the child, however that is defined. While the economic interests of children may be secured by maintaining a fluid relationship between work and school, compliance with social norms that place a reduced value on female education may also be factored in as securing the 'best interests' of female children. Evidence from both Africa and South Asia indicates that concerns for the safety of female children remain a paramount concern for many parents, focusing on fear of teenage pregnancy or culturally inappropriate interactions with male outsiders (Subrahmanian, 2002; Rose and Tembon, 1997).

Thus, while primary education is seen as a standard and acceptable requirement for everyday functioning, decisions about whether to educate children and, if so, which children, assume greater significance for different households based on considerations of 'affordability'. Affordability is not just a question of everyday financing of school participation, but also a medium- to long-term assessment of the returns to investment in education in relation to the social organisation of everyday life, livelihoods, marriage and family.

Jeffery and Jeffery (1998) argue that it is important to be aware of the *meaning* given to girls' schooling in different contexts in order to assess whether access to schooling is likely to have transformative effects on girls' and women's lives and lead to greater gender equality over their life-cycles. Generally, schooling reproduces gender ideologies, reinforcing gender discrimination in society rather than offering alternative ways of thinking about gender identities and inequalities. For girls, respectability and honour may be the key values reinforced; for boys, the assumption of their dominant economic role within the family, and hence greater entitlement to household resources, may go unchallenged.

Perceptions of a child's 'readiness' for school also affects household decision-making: in agrarian societies, parents assess the capacities of children in terms of their readiness to perform

... it is important to be aware of the meaning given to girls' schooling in different contexts in order to assess whether access to schooling is likely to ... lead to greater gender equality over their life-cycles.

Box 3.3 Disability: The Silent Exclusion

Children with disabilities are silently excluded from schooling and related opportunities. In poor families, in particular, where parents may choose among their children for investment in schooling, disabled children are likely to be by-passed. Disabled children who are able to participate in formal schools alongside their peers may be bullied or face abuse.

The intersections of gender and disability are likely to deepen this exclusion, with disabled girls having the least chance of making it to school. Cultural expectations that praise physical beauty or 'perfection' as a 'feminine' characteristic are likely to weigh harshly on disabled girls in particular, and result in the undervaluation of their contribution to family and society. Additional costs, such as access to special education programmes, medicines and extra health care costs, learning aids and equipment are also likely to constrain parental encouragement for disabled children to lead full lives.

Data remain poor on the types of disability and their correlation with participation in education. The UNESCO website suggests that in developing countries more than 90 per cent of children with disabilities do not attend school. Other estimates suggest that only 1 per cent of disabled women are literate compared with 3 per cent of disabled people as a whole (UNESCO, 2003).

The diversity of forms of disability is also a constraint on the development of clear policies for developing appropriate infrastructure and learning methods in public sector services. Data are usually not disaggregated, and the learning needs of different groups are therefore unknown to policy-makers. The World Health Organisation (WHO) has estimated that between 7–10 per cent of the total world population have some type of disability, 80 per cent of whom live in developing countries.

UNESCO, 2003

tasks, rather than on the basis of age. This can have an influence – and may also be gendered. Assessment of readiness can be based on physical growth (and hence the health status of children) and cognitive abilities (Fentiman *et al.*, 1999). This can be highly gendered where beliefs in the capacities of girls and women are already biased and they are judged to be of lower quality than boys. Sathar *et al.* (2003) note that in settings where parents invest unequally in their children for reasons based on age, sex, birth order or natural endowments, girls and boys may not be treated as exact substitutes, as they may be valued by parents for different reasons: 'A *"high-quality" girl may be different from a "high-quality" boy and may require different inputs'*.

Girls' socialisation into domestic roles is both a result of, and results in, wider gender inequalities.

Reproduction of Labour and its Relationship with Schooling

As noted earlier, female disadvantage in education is often explained in terms of the limited value placed on schooling for girls. In some cases, education can be seen as dangerous for females because it opens up alternative conceptions of society and feminine identity, and builds skills for achieving economic independence. The lack of attention paid to women's near-exclusive responsibility for the reproduction of life within the home results in the perpetuation of gender disadvantage. This manifests itself in the heavy participation of girls in domestic work relative to boys. Girls' socialisation into domestic roles is both a result of, and results in, wider gender inequalities.

Rapid increases in many parts of the world in the number of girls who attend school are the result of a combination of factors. Knodel (1997) points to the importance of recognising that socio-economic issues are key variables in determining education prospects, and to the role of rapid economic change and increasing urbanisation in promoting greater household investment in female education (Tansel, 1997). Macroeconomic incentives play a critical role in shaping household investment strategies. The impact of structural adjustment on African economies in the 1980s saw sharp decreases in the school enrolment of children in many countries of the region, as recession without safety nets and protection for household and state social sector expenditure reduced public

State policy or sensitive community development interventions can bring about changes in the factors that influence parental decision-making.

investment and put pressure on households to employ children in productive labour (UNICEF, 1998). In Thailand, on the other hand, gender equality in household education strategies reflects an awareness of the greater employment prospects for girls who have at least primary level education. Changes in the wider economy have had an impact on parental attitudes towards educating girls, and have positively influenced school attendance rates (Knodel, 1997).

In countries such as India (Kingdon, 1998) and Ethiopia (Rose and Al-Samarrai, 1997) the labour market provides little encouragement for increasing female education. Household aspirations for girls are constructed differently from those for boys as a result of prospects shaped by wider social and economic norms that establish appropriate behaviours and opportunities for women and men. Where boys are considered to be responsible for parental well-being, investment in them is seen as a rational decision, and cultural practices that reinforce the 'giving away' of girls in marriage are likely to serve as a disincentive for educating daughters. However, such practices are not static. State policy or sensitive community development interventions can bring about changes in the factors that influence parental decision-making.

Box 3.4 The Gendered Influence of Parents on Children

A study in rural Swaziland studied the impact of father migration on gender roles within the family and children's preparedness for and performance in school. When fathers migrated, there was no role model for boys and mothers found it hard to impose discipline, affecting their sons' academic performance. Boys from homes where fathers were absent were more likely to repeat grades than girls. Boys took over work in livestock maintenance, which affected their attendance and led to grade repetition. As fathers were more likely to be educated than mothers, the absence of a reading culture at home also affected children.

On the other hand, father absence served to show girls the risks of relying on spouses, as they witnessed the

---

> hardships endured by their mothers and the lack of reliable remittances. This led girls to view education as an important means of securing self-reliance in the future. Boys, on the other hand, dropped out early to follow their fathers into mining, for which completing education was not felt to be necessary.
>
> Kaabwe, 2000

Even where work is compatible with schooling, it remains an issue for policy-makers, as participation in work affects the quality of children's learning and their achievements.

Agricultural work on family land occupies a large proportion of working children; this work is often invisible owing to its seasonal nature and its partial compatibility with schooling; contrary to popular perception, parents are usually the employers, rather than entrepreneurs or corporations. Accordingly, the work participation rates of children tend to be higher in rural than in urban areas. Where wage labour markets are underdeveloped, as in Africa, children's waged work in urban areas and export-oriented industries is far less common than is often assumed (UNESCO, 2003).

> *A broad interpretation of the empirical literature suggests that the proportions in work and out of school are larger for girls than for boys in Asia, the proportion in work but not necessarily the proportion out of school is larger for boys than for girls in Latin America, and the proportion of boys and girls in work is roughly similar in most parts of Africa, although the girls who are out of school comprise a significant majority.* UNESCO, 2003: 122

Even where work is compatible with schooling, it remains an issue for policy-makers, as participation in work affects the quality of children's learning and their achievements. In particular, the long hours girls put into domestic work and the demands on their time that mark the daily routines of household management can be tiring and prevent them from focusing on their studies at any fixed time of day. Gender differentials underscore the phenomenon of child labour. Girls are often engaged in wage labour even where their income contribution is not critical to household subsistence, as evidence from Pakistan shows (Bhalotra, 2000). This demonstrates the extent to which girls' work is either a reflection of socialisation

Child labour is often compatible with schooling, because it contributes towards its costs.

or a default option – i.e. something girls do until they are married. The socialisation effect is also evident in the gender segmentation of work, with girls generally involved in cooking, cleaning and the care of siblings, and boys in collecting firewood, tending grazing animals and other activities outside the house.

Child labour is often compatible with schooling, because it contributes towards its costs. The costs of schooling for households are particularly high for poorer households (Rose and Al-Samarrai, 1997; Tansel, 1997; Knodel, 1997) and increase with higher levels of schooling. Direct costs (books, transport and clothing) remain high despite state subsidy in most countries, and in many areas distance from school remains a major constraint. The worlds of work and school are not always polarised choices for poor households. The phenomenon of children working to pay the costs of their schooling has also been noted in Ethiopia (Rose and Al-Samarrai, 1997) and India (Nieuwenhuys, 1994), although Rose and Tembon (1997), Oxaal (1997) and Colclough *et al.* (2003) point to the probability that girls' lack of control over their incomes, when they are engaged in waged work, may mean that their earnings are diverted to other household costs, including their brothers' schooling.

Boys' labour, particularly in pastoral societies such as those of Southern Africa, may be in demand or cause high levels of out-migration; in these contexts gender disparities are reversed in favour of girls (Mturi, 2003). However, Mturi also notes that diminishing returns to mining may mean that boys go back to school and lead to a closing of the reverse gender gap.

Box 3.5 Invisible Forms of Child Labour: The Practice of Child Fostering in Sub-Saharan Africa

The practice of fostering, studied particularly in West Africa, is on the increase, as families bear the brunt of HIV/AIDS. For girls, fostering may be a result of the demand for domestic labour; for boys, it may reflect a concern with improving their schooling and life opportunities. This is particularly true of urban areas, where households take foster children, and especially boys, into their care to socialise them and enrol them in school. The fostering of girl children, however, is often to supplement household labour. As Hashim (2005) points out for Ghana, the irony is that fostering young girls for domestic labour may help address shortages of domestic labour in urban households where girls are enrolling in schools in greater numbers. The relationship between the custody of very young children and housework indicates labour supply problems also in households where both spouses work outside the home and in female-headed households. A previous study based on Togo's 1981 census data revealed that female-headed households were more likely to host children, with a proportion of foster children nearly twice as high as that observed in male-headed households (29.5 compared with 15.8 per cent) (Pilon, 2003).

Fentiman *et al.* (1999) find that the migration and fostering of children is widespread in the poorer areas of Ghana and that it reflects regional inequalities. The outward migration of children is driven by the search for wage employment and schooling. Sometimes children pay for their schooling through working for kin, or they receive schooling as a form of 'compensation' for their labour. The linking of work with education in a context of migration and fostering is, however, a unreliable strategy as far as schooling is concerned – changes in the demand for labour in the foster home could push a foster child out of both home and education (Hashim, 2005).

Lack of a school in some villages often drives the practice of fostering. However, these children still suffer education inequalities in the urban areas: studies show that in many countries where fostering is a common practice, children living without their parents, particularly girls, have lower enrolment rates than the household heads' own offspring (ibid., 2005).

Conclusion

Many of the factors that reproduce childhood poverty and educational deprivation are reproduced through intergenerational transfers of deprivation. Educated parents are more likely to invest in their children's education; educated mothers, in particular, are likely to encourage their daughters' schooling. Even where mothers are uneducated, aspirations for a better life for their daughters often motivate them to want their daughters to attend school. However, frequently mothers are lone voices and need support and resources if they are to have a say in household decision-making. Investing in adult women, particularly in their empowerment, can complement strategies to support the schooling of daughters.

The following investments are also likely to have a strongly supportive impact on sustaining the demand for girls' schooling:

- Investments in reproductive health awareness and facilities for young girls to enable them to enjoy good health and a delayed age of pregnancy;

- Work with communities to raise awareness about the importance of female education in general, through implementing legal rights and creating forums for women to collectively address commonly experienced injustices;

- Ensuring the spread of early childhood care and education programmes and crèche facilities to allow young girls to be free from the responsibility of looking after their siblings;

- Proactive public action to promote female schooling through incentive programmes that are well-resourced and effectively targeted.

4. Supply-side Constraints on Girls' Schooling

Education systems perform several key roles in a child's life. Schools provide a central learning and socialisation experience; they are also an important counterpart to the family. They must therefore work alongside the families of their pupils to help build the capacities and skills of all learners, however different they may be from each other. This approach to education does not work in mass school systems which are under great pressure to show results that conform to national and regional standards. However, for all children and their parents, the experience of schooling is a critical determinant of their future. Where schools fail to inspire confidence in learners, especially first-generation learners, an important opportunity is lost.

For educators, reforming schools to ensure quality universal education, while responding to diverse groups of learners, is a challenge because of the multiple components that constitute the school experience. Because schools are such an important space for children, who are both psychologically and physically vulnerable, many demands are made of them. Schools must be safe; they must be clean; they must look after the health and nutrition of students, whose needs may not be met at home. They must provide learning and skills, and foster students' self-esteem, dignity, right not to be discriminated against, moral values and citizenship. For this, schools need to offer top quality services at low cost, reach out to parents and communities, follow up every child's attendance and performance, counsel children who have personal problems and offer them support. This agenda is a challenging one, but it is one that must be met. Strong supply-side policy frameworks are essential for schools to be valued as primary social institutions, recognising the strong overlaps between school and community on the one hand, and school and home on the other.

Investment in quality schooling for girls can help to even out social inequalities in the value accorded to girls and boys. In many communities where girls are unable to enrol in or

... for all children and their parents, the experience of schooling is a critical determinant of their future.

... the role of schooling in reproducing gender inequalities needs to be thoroughly examined.

attend school, there is differential valuation of the abilities of boys and girls, as shown in Chapter 3. Therefore, supply can and must play a critical role in reducing the scope for differential valuation of boys and girls to translate into differential investment in their schooling. Ensuring accessible schools of good quality can make a big contribution to redressing these biases. As Chapter 1 argues, it is not primary schooling that presents the biggest obstacle to gender equity in schooling, but the transition from primary to upper primary and secondary school that are the weakest links in girls' educational progress. Securing these transition points by investing in more schools, better financing and subsidies for girls and other disadvantaged children, secure transportation, quality teaching and educational support are all important aspects of supply.

Reproducing Society through the Education System

Education is one of the key sites where different ideologies reflecting dominant power structures are played out. While it has often been asserted that schooling offers space for both the reproduction and the contestation of these dominant forms of knowledge production, its role in reproducing gender inequalities needs to be thoroughly examined. This raises the 'schooling for subordination' hypothesis put forward by many feminists, who raise the concern that the question 'education for what?' is not part of the international debate on education and gender equality. Attention to processes of curriculum transaction and the hidden and 'evaded' curricula (American Association of University Women, 1992) have all taken second place in policy discourse to discussions about resourcing and establishing schools. Where educational provision is not informed by gender-aware analysis, the likelihood that state investment in education will itself exacerbate gender biases and gender discrimination is high. In particular, questions about the gender-equitable impacts of budgetary allocations and planning priorities need to be placed at the heart of gender-aware strategies for education for all. Subjecting policy choices to rigorous scrutiny through a gender lens is therefore important.

The Schooling Experience: Gender-based Violence

Recent efforts to universalise education need to be understood in terms of the processes of social change that they are unleashing. In many countries girls are being given access to what is essentially a public space where they can participate equally alongside men. This makes the school a fundamentally important space for the achievement of gender equality and the right to non-discrimination. However, in many cases, possibly because of the kind of social transformation that is being put in motion, schools are also sites of gender-based backlash. Violence against girls in school is one manifestation of the entrenched norms that hold girls back, and reinforces messages about their rightful place and role in society.

Although gender-based violence is often not reported as such and therefore is not considered differently from other forms of violence in schools, there is no doubt that it is linked to a range of problems in developing countries, such as under-achievement and high pupil drop-out. A report on sexual violence in South African schools (Human Rights Watch, 2001) found that the threat of violence at school is one of the most significant challenges to learning for children. Other reports corroborate this, and note the failure of educational systems to address the problem adequately. In Zimbabwe, Ghana and Malawi, according to a recent study (Leach *et al.*, 2003b), high levels of sexual aggression from boys, and sometimes teachers, against junior secondary girls go largely unpunished.

... the threat of violence at school is one of the most significant challenges to learning for children.

> **Box 4.1 Evidence of School-based Violence in Different Settings**
>
> In two reviews by Leach *et al.* (2003a; 2003b), the following findings from studies around the world are reported:
>
> - Twenty per cent of the 240 violent incidents reported in schools in and around Addis Ababa in 1996 were attempted rape.
>
> - A study in 1998 of a nationally representative sample of 11,735 South African women aged 15–49 found that

33 per cent of the 159 women who had been raped as children (under the age of 15) had been raped by teachers. Young girls are increasingly targeted in places where HIV/AIDS prevalence is high because they are seen to be free of the AIDS virus; the myth that sex with a virgin cures AIDS has led to the rape of very young infants.

- A 2001 study analysed reported incidents of child abuse by teachers in Zimbabwe, covering sexual, physical and emotional abuse. Of 246 reported cases of abuse by teachers in secondary schools between 1990 and 1997, 65.6 per cent involved sexual intercourse with pupils, 1.9 per cent involved rape or attempted rape and the remainder were cases of inappropriate teacher conduct (writing love letters, fondling, kissing or showing pornographic material to pupils).

- A survey in Ghana of violence against women and adolescent girls reported that 49 per cent of the 481 adolescent girls surveyed had been touched against their will at some time in their lives: 12 per cent of the offenders were pupils and 2 per cent were teachers. Four per cent of sexual assaults on adolescent girls were by fellow pupils and 2 per cent by teachers.

- In Latin America, the World Bank country study of Ecuador (2000) reports that 22 per cent of adolescent girls were victims of sexual abuse in an educational setting.

- An under-reported area of school-based gender violence is that which targets gays, lesbians and pupils of 'alternative' sexuality, as reported by a Human Rights Watch and International Gay and Lesbian Human Rights Commission report (2003), which found such violations in several African countries.

The predominance of findings from African countries is the result of imbalances in the research. Little work has been done in this area and evidence from around the world is thin: but the prevalence of violence and its impact on girls' education and on all children's school experience points to the importance of studying the prevalence of gender-based violence in other regions and settings.

Explicit gender violence is chiefly sexual violence, but other forms ... can be gender specific.

Explicit gender violence is chiefly sexual violence, but other forms, such as unregulated and excessive corporal punishment, bullying and physical assault, sometimes with guns and knives, verbal abuse and teachers' use of pupils for free labour can be gender specific. Aggressive and intimidating behaviour, unsolicited physical contact such as touching and groping, assault, coercive sex and rape all constitute abuse, as does any sexual relationship formed by a teacher with a pupil. In most contexts, this kind of relationship is a disciplinary offence against the teacher's conditions of employment and/or a criminal offence, when the student is a minor. These teachers and others working in a professional capacity with children are exploiting their position of authority and failing in their duty of care. Violence against girls in schools takes place in school toilet facilities, empty classrooms and corridors, hostel rooms and dormitories. Sexual abuse also takes place outside the school, occurring when schoolgirls form relationships with adult men who engage in transactional sex in exchange for gifts or money (Wood and Jewkes, 1997). The impact of sexual violence on girls' vulnerability to AIDS requires critical attention.

Teachers as Shapers of Gender Equality

Evidence suggests that efforts at the national level to tackle teacher misconduct are patchy. Studies from sub-Saharan Africa indicate that prosecutions of teachers for sexual assault or rape are rare, that those that are followed up take years to go through the courts and that they often end in dismissal. South Africa is tackling this by amending employment legislation to make sexual abuse of students a sackable offence. Generally, though, lack of political will seems to be the main problem. Power hierarchies within schools prevent accurate reporting, as solutions are most likely to be found in 'hushing it up'. As for sanctions against students, although girls who become pregnant generally have to leave school, boys who are guilty of sexual misconduct are rarely required to do so, even in countries such as Botswana, where there is policy that they should.

Box 4.2 Gender Division of Labour in Classroom Tasks

A recent study in Ghana and Botswana uncovered a wide range of institutional practices which reinforce and perpetuate the gendered nature of schooling. In 12 junior secondary schools studied in both countries, both male and female students and teachers were found to be performing primarily gender-specific duties, which for both female teachers and students were an extension of household tasks. Although prefects and monitors were appointed equally by gender, in practice there was an explicit gender hierarchy in which the male prefect dominated. In terms of general school duties, in all the schools in both countries girls were usually responsible for cleaning classrooms and offices, and for fetching water. Boys did weeding, picked up papers, cleaned windows and performed heavier duties like tree cutting. They were rarely observed using brooms or mops. Boys also tended to have a supervisory role, for example inspecting the plots rather than cleaning them. Whereas in some instances girls helped boys, for example by raking and bagging weeds for them to take to the dump, boys did not help girls. These findings obtained across both countries, even though Botswana has a much smaller gender gap than Ghana, and across schools, regardless of their academic achievements, and location, pointing to the entrenched biases in institutional practices.

Dunne and Leach, 2005

Ensuring gender parity of teachers can only partially contribute to the wider goal of ensuring gender parity in schools. Teachers' own behaviour is a critical part of the education process that needs to be tackled. Often teachers are found to deepen existing discrimination by overlaying their own biases onto existing social divisions and hierarchies. For example, teachers often differentiate between boys and girls and between social groups when apportioning tasks within the classroom: for example, girls are asked to clean schools and fetch water, and boys are required to clear bushes, cut grass and carry bricks. In Malawi, a study showed that girls were sometimes expected to substitute for male teachers' wives when they were away, performing tasks such as cleaning the house, fetching water and pounding maize (Colclough *et al.*, 2003).

Teachers may discriminate against their own daughters within the home, as data from Bangladesh show (Fransman *et al.*, 2003), and this behaviour may be reflected in the school setting, where they may enforce different disciplinary codes for girls and boys. Lessons observed in Jamaican schools were characterised by a lack of praise from teachers for boys, and teachers gave boys a disproportionate number of reprimands. A significant number of former students claimed that girls were given better treatment and sometimes escaped punishment that would have been meted out had the offender been a boy.

The 'Hidden Curriculum'

Sensitising teachers and alerting them to the implications of gender differentiation in the classroom is unlikely to make a significant difference if the curriculum remains gender biased. Getting the *curriculum* 'right' is important, although extremely challenging. In some countries, parents will not send their daughters to school if they feel that the curriculum is teaching them ideas that do not conform to prevailing social norms. In Guinea, parents perceived subjects such as home economics, childcare, sewing, gardening and handicrafts as important for girls and criticised their absence from the curriculum (Colclough *et al.*, 2003). This phenomenon is not restricted to 'traditional' societies: in France, a report published in 1997 by two parliamentarians noted the under-representation of women in teaching materials and expressed concern that where they were present, their roles were reduced to the social roles of mothers and wives, with implications for the kinds of role models that young girls were being offered, despite two decades of policy concern about gender bias in textbooks (Baudino, 2003).

Sexism in textbooks therefore needs fundamental atten-

Getting the curriculum 'right' is important, although extremely challenging.

... the issue is not merely about changing gender stereotypes in the nature of examples used, although that is a first step towards removing gender bias. Attention must also be paid to the silences in the curriculum about gender inequality.

tion, but the issue is not merely about changing gender stereotypes in the nature of examples used, although that is a first step towards removing gender bias. Attention must also be paid to the silences in the curriculum about gender inequality, or what is termed by researchers in the US as the 'evaded curriculum' (American Association of University Women, 2002).

The experience of 'transitional' countries in Central/South-eastern Europe is salutary. Now facing reversals in their overall educational situation, these countries are grappling with falls in gender parity. While women made rapid gains under socialist governments, particularly in respect of employment equity, less attention was paid to gender equity within the family, with underlying ideologies of gender difference remaining relatively untouched. There were very few examples of men involved in domestic activity in textbooks (Magno *et al.*, 2002). The result is that domestic work, including the care of children, is presented as women's work and inappropriate for men. Ideas of what constitute appropriate gender roles extend into the depiction of career choices for girls and boys. In most countries of the region, textbooks present boys and girls with an artificially limited selection of occupations regarded as appropriate for their gender. Both boys and girls may suffer if they only consider these occupations, rather than basing their choices on their needs, preferences and aptitudes. However, the impact is much more serious for girls, because they are usually associated with low-paid and low-prestige occupations. For example, primary school textbooks in Romania depict women as 'school teachers, villagers, fruit or flower sellers, while men are viewed as astronauts, policemen, physicians, actors, conductors, and masons ...' Thus, girls are pushed towards 'easy and clean' professions from an early age, with well-defined responsibilities that facilitate and allow a 'normal' family life. Boys, however, are guided to technical and profitable careers that will enable them to support a family in the future (Magno *et al.*, 2002).

Boys and Girls in the Classroom: Gender Inequalities and Learning Outcomes

Evidence that girls are out-performing boys has created a stir in many countries, not least because it appears to confound typical assumptions about the nature of gender inequality. As with the data on gender disparities in favour of boys, though, careful treatment of the evidence is required to establish what performance indicators are capturing: in what contexts girls are out-performing boys; which girls are out-performing which boys; the institutional factors that may explain these differences; and the wider socio-cultural factors that may influence these differentials. In some countries, for example Australia, the rise of a 'what about the boys?' discourse is seen to represent an early backlash against gains made by girls in education (Blackmore, 2004). However, evidence of girls performing better than boys does not reflect a reversal of gender equality as is sometimes suggested, but indicates changes in patterns of gender differentiation.

The United Kingdom and France are both countries where the relative under-performance of boys has received much attention. Recent reports from the UK Department for Education reflect this concern. In 2001, 56.5 per cent of girls achieved five or more General Certificate of Secondary Education (GCSE) or equivalent passes, compared to 45.7 per cent of boys. The proportion of girls and boys achieving top grades at 18 appears to be broadly equal, although girls seem to be gaining a slight advantage (Arnot and Phipps, 2003). In France, girls' pass rates are equal to or marginally better than boys in all subjects, including mathematics. The gap narrows from several percentage points in French to a few tenths of a point in mathematics, but it is always in favour of girls. Girls are also performing better than boys. Only 40 per cent of children leaving school without qualifications are girls. In terms of grades, 15.3 per cent of girls achieve grades 'A' and 'B' compared to just 12.6 per cent of boys (Baudino, 2003). In the UK, girls' better relative performance in examinations at age 16 is a recent phenomenon, achieved over the last ten years. This new pattern of access and achievement has also been the result of boys' failure to improve their performance at the same rate as girls from a very young age, particularly in language and reading (Arnot and Phipps, 2003).

The Caribbean region is also well-known for girls' better performance, having closed the gender gap before the beginning of the 1990s, and maintaining gender parity over the decade. In the Caribbean, on average, girls start schooling earlier, attend school more regularly, drop out of school more

... evidence of girls performing better than boys does not reflect a reversal of gender equality as is sometimes suggested, but indicates changes in patterns of gender differentiation.

infrequently, stay in school longer and achieve higher levels of functional education at the end of their schooling than boys. Whatever progress has been made in literacy in the Caribbean, women have made more progress than men and are on the whole more literate (Miller, 2000).

Box 4.3 **Gender Patterns in Educational Achievement**

A review of the available evidence (UNESCO, 2003) shows several different patterns:

- In Costa Rica, girls fail less than boys at primary and secondary levels, though this reverses in night schools;

- In Hungary, girls participate more in academic contests during secondary school years and gain better grades than boys;

- In other countries of the former Soviet bloc, achievement rates for boys and girls widen in favour of boys progressively through the system – at grade 4, boys only outperform girls in some subjects (mathematics and science), but the gap widens significantly in the upper grades and the last year of secondary school;

- In Chile, pass rates are higher for girls than boys in both secondary and basic education, and drop-out rates are lower);

- In Bangladesh, results for boys and girls are mixed – boys do better in most subjects, while girls do better in English. However, in some subjects differences are statistically insignificant;

- In Ethiopia, some subjects reveal wider gender gaps in performance than others, notably mathematics, in an educational system where aggregate achievement for boys is slightly higher than for girls, though with regional variations. Gaps between boys and girls widen through the system – in 2000/01 only 20 per cent of girls passed the grade 10 examinations compared to

---

53 per cent of boys, and 46 per cent and 67 per cent, respectively, passed the grade 12 examinations.

- In Togo, both boys and girls fare poorly at school, but the impact of girls' failure is more negative, as parents are less tolerant of successive grade repetition by their daughters and are therefore quicker to withdraw them following poor performance.

UNESCO, 2003

Several factors are cited to explain the factors that shape the different performance of girls and boys, and these vary in different contexts. Explanatory factors refer in various ways to the construction of masculine and feminine gender identities and the impact this has on school performance. In Jamaica and Chile, it is hypothesised that there are differences in motivation levels and attitudes. For example, in Jamaica, it is widely speculated that early patterns of 'male privilege' (less supervision and fewer home responsibilities) contribute to perceived patterns of greater compliance by girls with school expectations (following orders, routines, completing work), and thus better academic results (Sewell et al., 2003).

In the UK, policy reform has contributed greatly to closing gender gaps in parity and fostering a greater culture of equality between males and females. This is also the case in France. Education policy reforms do not, however, in all cases result in the closing of gender gaps in learning and performance. Jamaica offers an interesting and paradoxical case. A recent study reveals that despite tremendously positive investment in the education sector and high enrolment rates in lower secondary education, there is low learning, interest and participation on the part of boys (Sewell et al., 2003). Numerous reasons are put forward to explain male under-performance in the Caribbean. These focus on the socialisation patterns of boys and girls and the differences inherent in these. For example, Figueroa (2000) argues that the privilege men have always exerted over women has come at a price. The privileging of male gender is reflected in different ways: men have occupied

Ensuring that girls have as much freedom to access subjects and skills conventionally understood to be more appropriate for boys and men is one aspect of change that is required to promote gender equality through education.

a wider social space, controlled more resources, maintained a higher social position and exercised greater power.

The relative under-performance of boys in Jamaica and other Caribbean countries within this historical context of male privilege is important to understand. The phenomenon offers many insights into the social construction of masculine identity and the damaging effects of failing to pay attention to the socialisation of boys. Thus gendered patterns are found in the nature of household chores, degree of parental supervision, severity of discipline and punishment, and expectations in relation to sexuality. Girls tend to be more closely supervised by parents and given more encouragement to perform well at school; this is positively reinforced by teachers, who tend to view boys as less motivated and hence less interested in education. The ways in which schools reinforce or challenge wider social norms are also an important part of the explanation. The link between the home and the school becomes apparent, as does the influence of wider processes of gender inequality and their impact on education (Sewell *et al.*, 2003).

Ensuring that girls have as much freedom to access subjects and skills conventionally understood to be more appropriate for boys and men is one aspect of change that is required to promote gender equality through education. Another is to expose boys to skills in management of the reproductive sphere, known as 'home economics'. Ansell (2002) argues that the decline of home economics teaching in rural schools in Lesotho and South Africa, partly on grounds that these are stereotypical 'female' activities, deprives both girls and boys of important skills and diminishes the importance given to tasks carried out in the reproduction of family and home.

Box 4.4 Single Sex Schools

School choice is not just about choices between schools in the state and non-state sectors. Other policy choices that have implications for resource allocation include the issue of co-educational versus single-sex schools. This question continues to demand policy and research attention.

In many developing countries, single-sex learning environments are considered particularly important for post-primary school learners, where co-educational education may be considered a risky proposition and a disincentive to continue girls' schooling, in particular, in the context of adolescence and the onset of sexual maturation. Single-sex classrooms and schools may be attractive to parents and educators as a way of minimising distractions for girls and boys, especially as they grow older.

In many developing countries, modern education built on the foundations of traditional schooling, where content was sex differentiated. For example, in traditional African education, boys were taught different things from girls because their adult roles were different (Kaabwe, 2000).

In developed countries, single-sex schools have been closed over time and co-educational schools have become the norm. In the 1960s and 1970s in the USA, for example, single-sex schools were seen as a barrier to the socialisation of girls and boys. However, there is now a renewed debate over whether boys and girls learn better in a single-sex environment. In the USA, a recent proposal to offer a single-sex environment alongside an equivalent co-educational option has intensified debate. 241 public schools in the USA now offer some single-sex classrooms, up from three in 1995, according to the National Association for Single Sex Public Education (NASSPE). Of these, 51 are completely single-sex schools. NASSPE argues that, contrary to conventional wisdom, co-educational settings reinforce gender stereotypes via the process of 'gender intensification', whereby boys and girls absorb and reflect deeply held stereotypes about the abilities and inclinations of the opposite sex. NASSPE argues that there are three categories of advantage of single-sex education for girls: (i) expanded educational opportunity through exposure to non-traditional subjects and activities; (ii) custom-tailored learning and instruction based on different learning styles; and (iii) greater autonomy, especially in relationships, evidenced in lower rates of unwanted and teenage pregnancy.

The research is mixed and suggests that single-sex education can provide benefits to some students under certain circumstances. Earlier efforts to link differential achievements of girls and boys in co-educational versus single-sex environments have courted controversy through attributions to sex-specific learning style and brain growth. However, other studies suggest that race, class and other structural characteristics of society are far greater predictors of learning performance and achievement than sex, and that there are far more similarities than differences between girls and boys. There is also a concern that myths about sex-specific learning achievement patterns could actually influence the behaviour of girls and boys, reinforcing conventional wisdom that girls lag behind in maths and science, while boys struggle with reading and verbal skills.

Gender streaming is also being considered as a promising option for education in developing countries. Research from Uganda suggests that girls only schools and schools where girls form a significant majority of the student body are perceived to be more suitable for the development of female leaders than co-educational schools. The same is true of boys' leadership skills in boys only schools. When girls are elected to student bodies in co-educational schools, they struggle to prove their capability and their actions are subjected to intense scrutiny (Male, 2000). Single-sex school attendance was found to benefit girls in maths in Nigeria, eliminating the stereotypical view that girls cannot succeed at mathematics (Kaabwe, 2000). Research in Pakistan and sub-Saharan Africa has also shown that single-sex education has a positive impact on enrolment and achievement (Kane, 2004).

Gender streaming within co-educational schools is also seen as a policy option, as it does not eliminate a co-educational environment, but allows for greater academic attention through single-sex classrooms.

Subject choices represent an interesting area of education that needs greater qualitative exploration. Baudino (2003) notes that in France, despite the fact that girls out-perform boys at secondary school, their immediate post-secondary choices reveal a marked pattern in favour of higher education, rather than professional training, such as the law or the civil service. In Chile, a study conducted in 2002 showed that despite achieving better results than men at secondary school, women did not perform as well in the university selection test. A comparison of a cohort of students who took a school test in 1998 and a university selection test in 2002 found that the low results of women in the latter bore no relation to their achievement at school. One explanation provided was motivation – males were more concerned to make sure they achieved the scores needed to enter the university's prestigious programmes and hence took crash courses to prepare for entrance tests (Avalos, 2003). Aspirations and performance in post-education entrance examinations and tests may thus run counter to the performance of girls in school.

Choices of particular subjects or specialisations reflect the wider point that boys see the world of work as their dominant opportunity and are keen to enter it early; on the other hand, girls are more likely to want to stay on in higher education in order to compete in the labour market. This may suggest that labour market discrimination drives greater gender parity, but this is not the case. In Togo, for example, the lack of employment for women, and the scarcity of jobs for diploma holders since the implementation of economic reforms, has meant that consciously or otherwise young girls anticipate being denied access to employment and prepare themselves for entry, at a very young age, into the informal sector. Field research in Togo shows that this leads both girls and their parents to consider schooling for girls as 'useless' (Lange, 2003).

Where specialisation is encouraged by the structure of the education system, gender tracking becomes more apparent, and in many countries tends to be the rule rather than the exception. In the UK, although the gap between boys and girls in subject choice is closing, largely owing to the introduction of reforms that have resulted in a common examination and common curriculum for all students, women and men still choose sex-stereotyped subjects at higher levels. Gender stereo-

Choices of particular subjects ... reflect the wider point that boys see the world of work as their dominant opportunity ... on the other hand, girls are more likely to want to stay on in higher education in order to compete better in the labour market.

typing is as prevalent at degree level as at other levels, with men being over-represented in engineering and technology and women over-represented in education and the humanities (Arnot and Phipps, 2003). The Equal Opportunities Commission (EOC) has also reported that youth training and modern apprenticeship schemes display gender stereotyping of occupations (EOC, 1998, cited in ibid.).

Box 4.5 **Gender Differences in Learners' Aspirations – Some Global Findings**

The Programme for International Student Assessment (PISA) is an initiative covering 28 OECD and 15 non-OECD countries aimed at measuring how well prepared are young adults at age 15 (when they are approaching the end of compulsory schooling) to meet the challenges of today's knowledge societies.

The data in the PISA survey explored students' expected occupations and found that the occupations that students expect to have at the age of 30 seem to predict the career choices they make later on. Female students in the participating countries were far more likely than males to report expected occupations related to life sciences and health, including medicine, biology, nutrition and teaching. Male students were more likely to expect careers associated with physics, mathematics or engineering. Given the effects of gender-stereotyped expectations, the report argues that education systems should embrace the policy objective of 'moderat-ing gender differences in occupational expectations – and to the extent that these are related to gender patterns in student performance and student interest – reduce performance gaps in different subject areas'.

A deeper underlying reason for differences in subject choice may also be that female students dominate academic streams in some countries in order to compensate for gender-based hidden or explicit discrimination in the labour market. Sex-based segregation and discrimination combine to give women unequal access to economic opportunities relative to men. Gaps in employment, wages and political representation keep women in positions of relative disadvantage, inadequately reflecting what women and girls achieve within education when they are given opportunities. Despite concern about male under-achievement, which is a serious issue meriting attention in some contexts, it is clear that society has different expectations for males and females. The under-achievement of males in the educational arena has not resulted in their parallel under-achievement in the economic and political spheres. Women often require higher levels of attainment than men to compete for jobs, receive equal remuneration, obtain decision-making positions and gain access to an equal share of productive resources (Bailey, 2003).

However, a key factor determining access to employment is not educational attainment, but access to vocational courses. A survey of Asian countries' performance in relation to gender equity shows that higher rates of unemployment prevail for women at all levels, but particularly in some countries. For instance, in Indonesia and Sri Lanka, both countries with relatively good gender parity in education, unemployment rates for women are higher than those for men across all levels of education. The Indonesian figures show that the higher a woman's level of education, the higher the rate of unemployment. The highest rates of unemployment are among those with general upper secondary and university education. Choosing a vocational stream of secondary education may offer women a better chance of employment. Although this phenomenon applies to both genders, educated females are more vulnerable to unemployment: their unemployment rates at diploma and university levels are over twice those of males. Even so, there is not necessarily parity in the opportunities offered to women and men with vocational education. In Indonesia, women with vocational education are more likely to be unemployed than men (Lee, 2002).

A study carried out by the Economic Commission for Latin America and the Caribbean (ECLAC) in 1995 (ECLAC and UNIFEM, 1995) shows that women in the Caribbean need to have four more years of schooling than men in order to compete for comparable salaries. In Chile, women with secondary

Gaps in employment, wages and political representation continue to keep women in positions of relative disadvantage, inadequately reflecting what women and girls are achieving within education when they are given opportunities.

In areas where jobs have been created, women have been concentrated in low-paid public services such as education, medical services and culture.

education or less are employed mostly in domestic work, as office workers and in diminishing numbers in the textile industry, whereas men with secondary education or less are employed in industry, building, agriculture, vehicle driving, forestry and fishing (MIDEPLAN, 2002, cited in Avalos, 2003). Despite consistently higher levels of education, women earn less than men in many countries of Central and Eastern Europe and the former Soviet Union. At the end of the 1990s, female wages constituted 79 per cent of male wages in Poland; 72 per cent in Ukraine; and 53 per cent in Azerbaijan. In Romania, the gap between women and men's pay grew in almost every sector of the economy during the transition period. In public administration, which employs a high proportion of women, women's average monthly earnings fell from 85 to 78 per cent of those of men between 1994–98. In areas where jobs have been created, women have been concentrated in low-paid public services such as education, medical services and culture. The impact of the decline of the public sector on employment opportunities has been particularly harsh in some countries. In Togo, the lack of policies geared to women's employment in the context of a shrinking public sector has not only enlarged the gender gap to the disadvantage of female teachers at all levels, but has also done so within the education ministry, where the gender parity index is 0.26 in favour of men, the worst of any government department (Lange, 2003).

Policy Issues

Poor quality supply can exacerbate demand-side constraints to female schooling, and strategies for improving supply require a concerted and holistic approach, rather than piecemeal efforts to address specific aspects of demand-side constraints. For example, Eloundou-Enyegue (2004) shows for Cameroon that reducing the incidence of pregnancy-related school drop-outs would significantly reduce, and possibly close, the country's gender gap in the completion of secondary school, but goes on to argue that the impact would be stronger if policy-makers addressed other sources of gender inequality, including improving secondary school access for girls.

In other words, planners must first consider other discriminatory forces that operate before the onset of puberty and outside the realm of pregnancy. (Ibid.: 525)

School infrastructure

Expanding the availability and improving the infrastructure of schooling

Expanding the availability of schools is clearly a first step towards universalising education. The constraints placed on the mobility of girls, because of both perceived and real physical risks, as well as in traditional settings where the free movement of girls runs counter to cultural norms, are primary issues in any universal education system. In many countries rapid strides have been made towards gender parity in primary schooling merely by increasing the availability of schools. In places where restricted mobility is a factor preventing girls from using public transport to attend school after the primary stage, the availability of higher primary and secondary schooling in the vicinity of villages is essential. However, in many countries post-primary level schooling is widely dispersed, and distances between villages and higher level schools increase (Tansel, 1997; Knodel, 1997). This has negative impacts for girls.

Two challenges remain. First, schools must be available to diverse populations, particularly those in remote areas and groups who may be excluded from policy consideration because of their marginal or minority status. Infrastructure development in the form of roads and bridges is critical to reduce the time taken to reach school in areas where the building of new schools is hampered by terrain or climate. Ensuring that resource allocations are free from regional or social bias is a necessary corollary to increased investment in building schools. Equity in the availability of schools is important, but it is difficult to obtain aggregate data. Second, the expansion of upper primary/ lower secondary and higher secondary schools remains a challenge. Securing equity in the transition between primary and higher levels of schooling was identified in Chapter 1 as a key policy issue for girls' education. In order to make this transition easier and reduce the drop-out rate, the availability of afford-

... schools must be available to diverse populations, particularly those in remote areas and groups who may be excluded from policy consideration because of their marginal or minority status.

able and quality secondary schooling has to be expanded, and measures to make available safe and affordable, if not cost-free, transportation are essential.

> **Box 4.6 Reducing the Distance between Home and School in India**
>
> India's rapid progress towards universal access to primary education has been aided by an expansion in the number of schools. Between 1950/51 and 2002, the number of primary schools in India increased threefold, and the number of upper primary schools by 15 times. This has created a significant expansion of elementary education facilities, with a positive impact on school attendance among the eligible age group.
>
> Distance as a factor constraining attendance at school has therefore become less significant. According to National Sample Survey Organisation (NSSO) data for 1986–87, approximately 10 per cent of all children could not attend school because of non-availability of schools, while according to the 1995–96 survey only around 2 per cent of children were not attending school for this reason.

Under-investment in female schooling has particular implications for provision in countries where public schools are typically sex segregated. In such contexts, two schools are required for every point of access. An example of this is Pakistan, where an earlier policy practice was to build one girls' school for every two built for boys, based on assumptions about the demand for girls' schooling (Lloyd *et al.*, 2002).

Hostels and residential schools for girls can also go a long way in enabling girls to move beyond primary schooling and attend secondary and higher education institutions. Safety is a primary concern; poorly secured premises and lack of basic facilities reduce the efficacy of any investment in such institutions.

The availability of water and sufficient toilets for schoolchildren is an important supportive mechanism in sustaining school attendance. Girls, in particular, face significant problems where toilets are not available, particularly in their adolescent years. The availability of good clean water is essential for ensuring the health of learners. Privacy is also very important in toilet facilities for girls.

> ## Box 4.7 Girls' Schooling in Exceptional Circumstances: Conflict and Other Emergencies
>
> Much of the literature discussing gender and education issues presumes stable governance and other conditions, and the ability of children to access public education. However, increasingly children are going to school in situations of conflict and in the aftermath of devastation experienced as a result of both natural and man-made disasters.
>
> Conflicts and 'fragile states' result in the disruption of public services and the erosion of systems, with very little or no capacity development of teachers, curriculum, school infrastructure and textbooks. Civilian populations are often caught in the cross-fire of internal conflict or displaced from their homes, seeking shelter in refugee camps for long periods. This includes teachers, who during insurgencies and conflict may become messengers or hostages. Displacement caused by human and environmental disasters can destroy lives and livelihoods in ways that take years to rebuild, psychologically as well as economically. In all these situations, girls' education, already relatively devalued, suffers more than that of boys. Scarce resources are conserved for expenditure on boys and during the process of reconstruction responsibilities devolve even more on young women. There is often an intensification of sexual violence and early marriage practices. Societies facing severe disruption may cling deeply to tradition, with particular implications for opportunities for girls' and women's development and empowerment.
>
> Conflict, in particular, unleashes great damage on societies, not only destroying infrastructure such as schools, but placing civilian populations in situations

of stress and uncertainty. A recent estimate suggests that about 43 million of the 115 million children estimated to be out of school worldwide are children caught up in conflict situations (Save the Children, 2006). They may be killed, permanently disabled or injured, or psychologically scarred from having witnessed the excesses of war. Children may lose months and days, if not years, of their education. Girls in particular are disproportionately affected. Low levels of gender parity and adult female literacy are strongly correlated with conflict. Being caught in the cross-fire and exposed to health and survival risks also renders children's education vulnerable to disruption, and may result in parents' reluctance to continue their children's schooling. However, as UNESCO (2003) reports, parents often consider schooling the best prospect for restoring a sense of stability to children's lives in the midst of conflict. Education can thus play a preventive and protective role in relation to conflict – through building skills of conflict resolution, values of peace and tolerance, and acceptance of diversity, as well as the use of schools as rehabilitative spaces.

Children are often placed at the heart of conflicts, mobilised as soldiers or used as human shields. They are at risk of being abducted for forced recruitment as child soldiers. For example, it is estimated that in Nepal, between January and August 2005, more than 11,800 students were abducted from rural schools for indoctrination or forced recruitment into the militia (Save the Children, 2006). It is estimated that in the 1990s, approximately 100,000 girls directly participated in conflicts in at least 39 different countries (Kirk, 2003), particularly in civil wars and insurgencies. Kirk (ibid.) describes how the role played by girls is not just that of fighters, but also cooks, sex slaves, porters and spies. The post-conflict reintegration into school of young women who may have been sexually brutalised or are pregnant is often an invisible policy issue.

Emergencies, and the displacement they cause, lead to an intensification of gender differences in access to and participation in education, and thus require concerted action. Girls' access to schooling in these contexts is affected by issues of distance, concerns about safety, lack of female teachers willing to work in risky environments and intensification of domestic chores, and the chance of survival chances is severely compromised.

Amid the severe constraints placed on young people as a consequence of these disruptions, there are also opportunities for new beginnings. Societies which are engaged in reconstruction following conflict or disaster are often able to renegotiate new systems and social structures through proactive policy measures, or through processes of change initiated in communities that have experienced loss. New ways of living can be developed out of the experience of displacement. Schools in refugee camps can serve as channels for the generation of different kinds of information, including education about health and survival, and skills and values relating to conflict resolution. Camps for internally displaced persons (IDPs) can offer new services and opportunities. For example, in the camps set up as a result of the conflict in the Darfur region of Sudan many girls have gained access to education for the first time. Skills training programmes for girls and adult literacy classes for women also advance female education. The establishment of parent-teacher associations in these camps has created new interfaces between teachers and the community, and opportunities to support girls' education.

Natural disasters have similar consequences in terms of disrupting people's lives, although their duration and aftermath are traumatic in different ways. As with conflict, there are often signals or warnings that indicate the possibility of an emergency. Large-scale devastation is usually a result of natural disasters, resulting in loss of life, livelihoods and institutions. In such situations, as with conflict, the quick resumption of

... free education ... is narrowly defined in terms of tuition charges, obscuring the fact that the costs of uniforms, textbooks and stationery often add a more significant cost burden than tuition fees.

education services offers stability, as well as a daily rhythm to life that has restorative implications.

School costs

Proof that the costs of schooling, in the form of direct fees and indirect charges and costs, serve as a deterrent to universal education can be found in the huge spurts in enrolment in countries that have reduced charges or made schooling free (Tomasevski, 2006; UN Millennium Project, 2005). For example, countries that have free education policies in sub-Saharan Africa, even if these are only partial or recently introduced, have higher school enrolment rates than countries which do not. Uganda, Malawi, Tanzania and Kenya have all eliminated fees and cut the costs of schooling with positive results for enrolment. However, despite the announcement of free primary education in many countries, this is narrowly defined in terms of tuition charges, obscuring the fact that the costs of uniforms, textbooks and stationery often add a more significant cost burden than tuition fees. Tomasevski (2006) identifies 24 different charges imposed on learners and their families. Further, communities are often expected to contribute to the building of schools.

In many Asian developing countries, households meet a large proportion of education expenditure through 'unofficial' fees, even where official policy is to provide 'fee-free' primary schooling. Studies reviewed by Lewin (1998) indicate that a high proportion of expenditure on schooling comes from private sources – over 50 per cent in Vietnam and Cambodia, more than 20 per cent in Philippines and over 40 per cent in India. In addition, the opportunity costs of educating children where they make a contribution to the running of the household (whether in the reproductive or productive domains) add to the burdens that poor households, in particular, bear in providing education for their children.

High costs of schooling are likely to force parents to make choices about which children should receive the benefits of education, and therefore allow inherent biases to deepen, as noted in the previous chapter, thereby compromising government attempts to promote compulsory education. Parental calculations about the worth of a child are likely to be strongly

Table 4.1 Countries with Charges for Primary Education, by Region

Sub-Saharan Africa	Eastern Europe and Central Asia	Asia	Middle East and North Africa	Latin America	Caribbean
Angola	Albania	Bhutan	Djibouti	Bolivia	Antigua &
Benin	Armenia	Burma/Myanmar	Egypt	Colombia	Barbuda
Burkina Faso	Azerbaijan	Cambodia	Iran	Dominican	Belize
Cameroon	Belarus	China	Israel	Republic	Grenada
Central African Rep.	Bulgaria	Fiji Islands	Jordan	Ecuador	Guyana
Chad	Croatia	Indonesia	Lebanon	El Salvador	Haiti
Congo/Brazzaville	Georgia	Laos	Qatar	Guatemala	St Lucia
Congo/Kinshasa	Kazakhstan	Maldives	Sudan	Honduras	St Vincent
Cote d'Ivoire	Kyrgyzstan	Nepal	Syria	Nicaragua	Suriname
Equitoreal Guinea	Macedonia	Pakistan	Tunisia	Panama	Trinidad &
Eritrea	Moldova	Papua New	United Arab	Paraguay	Tobago
Ethiopia	Romania	Guinea	Emirates	Peru	
Gabon	Russia	Philippines	Yemen		
Ghana	Serbia	Singapore			
Guinea	Tajikistan	Vietnam			
Guinea-Bissau	Turkmenistan				
Mali	Turkmenistan	*Governments rolling*			
Mauritania	Uzbekistan	*back charges*			
Mozambique		Bangladesh			
Namibia		India			
Niger		Malaysia			
Senegal		Mongolia			
Togo					
Zimbabwe					

Governments rolling
back charges
Burundi
Gambia
Kenya
Lesotho
Liberia
Madagascar
Malawi
Nigeria
Rwanda
Sierra Leone
South Africa
Swaziland
Tanzania
Uganda
Zambia

Source: Tomasevski (2006)

... international experience shows that there is a potential trade-off between the quantity ... and quality of schooling, if governments fail to ensure that expansion of school facilities and quality teaching accompany demand-side reforms.

influenced by gender, as well as by the child's ability and inclination. School attendance is also affected by the vagaries of seasonal fluctuations in household income and can become impossible for children in the event of the death or ill-health of family members, crop failure and other unpredictable shocks. The large numbers of drop-outs bear testimony to the inability of poor children, in particular, to sustain attendance at school. Substantial reductions in the costs of education are a vital policy tool for bringing more children, particularly girls, into school.

Evidence from several countries shows that where public expenditure is squeezed, thus constraining the provision of universal free education, targeted financial assistance to girls and children from poor or other excluded groups is likely to have a positive impact. Assistance in the form of scholarships and stipends helps households allocate resources more effectively to support their children's schooling and can, if it is generous enough, cover the costs of attending school.

However, international experience shows that there is a potential trade-off between the quantity – greater numbers of children enrolled – and quality of schooling, if governments fail to ensure that expansion of school facilities and quality teaching accompany demand-side reforms. Poor people are not put off solely by the costs of schooling, but by a calculation of the returns to high costs in the form of quality education. Both costs *and* quality matter in parental decision-making, and it is unlikely that reducing the cost will be enough to prevent pupils from dropping out. Investment in quality education also means targeting resources at school improvement programmes at the same time as reducing costs to households.

School choice

Public schooling, particularly elementary education, remains a cornerstone of the 'public goods' discourse in education. Ensuring that the state provides quality education services for all has been integral to the idea of education as a 'right' (Tomasevski, 2006). In the context of the rapid expansion of mass education systems in the developing world, school choice has become a pertinent issue. The role of the private sector in bridging the gap between public investment and the demand for universal quality education is a contentious policy question.

Bennell (2003) points out the difficulty of estimating the scale and type of private provision for definitional as well as measurement reasons. He notes that as a result both of inflated government estimates of public school enrolment, as well as the largely 'unrecognised' nature of primary school private providers, official data on non-state providers are hard to obtain, although small-scale studies uncover a fairly robust pattern of growth of private providers in primary schooling. It is particularly important to distinguish among non-state providers in terms of commercial bodies, NGOs and community-based providers (such as faith-based organisations), but there is little official data except for schools which are registered with the state (thus making them eligible for state subsidies).

While the private sector is an increasingly significant player, Lewin (1998) notes that for Asia its role may be most attractive where *'public budgetary allocations are already high and unlikely to increase, where adequate income is available, and where equity is not unduly threatened'*. The equity implications of private sector involvement in supporting or supplementing public education require consideration, particularly in relation to increasing disparities between the poor and the better off, given that the latter may be more able and inclined to spend more of their household income on education. The implications for equity between girls and boys should also be considered, given that parents may be less willing to spend money on their daughters' schooling than on their sons'. Finally, there are implications for differentials between the more and less developed regions of a country, given that the former may attract greater private sector investment.

It is often argued that private schools expand the range of choice available to parents and place pressure on the public system to compete with private schools, thus offering better quality education. However, there is also evidence that where private schools become providers in competition with government schools, inequities emerge, with better-off children getting access to private schools and poor children, particularly girls, remaining in often poor quality public schools. There is also a concern that the creation of markets for schooling can reduce pressure on governments to provide good quality edu-

... where private schools become providers in competition with government schools, inequities emerge, with better-off children getting access to private schools and poor children, particularly girls, remaining in often poor quality public schools.

The spread of private schooling is particularly associated with countries where there is significant income inequality.

cation, and exacerbate such inequities. This is particularly the case for countries that have yet to achieve universal enrolment in elementary education, and where the coverage and quality of public schools remains underdeveloped.

Other arguments in favour of private schooling are that private schools are often more cost effective than public schools because they tend to be more efficiently managed. However, evidence from India suggests that a mix of public–private inputs may actually be more efficient and cost effective, with private schools which receive public support being the most cost effective (Colclough, 1997).

The increase in private sector enrolment is largely the result of growing parental demand for education, coupled with dysfunctional government schooling systems. In the absence of reforms to improve the quality of public schools, parents often 'vote with their feet' to opt for alternative providers, in the hope that the quality of education will be better. Plural forms of provision are also widely considered to have boosted access to schooling, particularly for poor households. Poor teacher motivation and performance are significant factors in persuading poor parents to send their children to non-state schools where they can manage to do so. Thus despite efforts to invest in public education systems, expanded physical access has not curbed the rise of alternative private sector provision.

The spread of private schooling is particularly associated with countries where there is significant income inequality. Enrolment in private primary schools as a proportion of total enrolment is especially high in South Asia, particularly in Pakistan and Bangladesh, but also in India. Studies from India also attest to the wide inequalities associated with plural provision – female and *dalit* (ex-untouchable) children were found to attend government schools, while boys and children from more privileged castes were more likely to attend private schools (PROBE, 1999). More recent data suggest that these gaps may be closing because of the failures of state-provided schooling to respond to changing educational demands (see Box 4.8). A study from Ghana shows that increases in female access to education were largely concentrated in low-quality schools, while a greater proportion of boys attended high status schools (Weis, 1981, cited in Saith and Harriss-White, 1998).

Box 4.8 The Spread of Private Schooling in India

A recent estimate based on a national survey in India (Pratham, 2005) provides some new data on the spread of private schooling and gender differentials in access to public and private schooling. These data are based on figures collected from 9,521 villages across 485 districts.

What is striking is that although there are gender differentials, the proportion of girls who attend private schools is not much lower than that of boys.

Age group	Children in different types of schools across India (%)	
	Government	Private
6–14 All	75.1	16.4
6–10 All	77.8	15.5
11–14 All	71.6	17.8
6–10 Boys	76.9	17.0
6–10 Girls	78.9	13.7
11–14 Boys	71.9	19.2
11–14 Girls	71.2	16.2

Pratham, 2005

Pluralism ... and diversity of types of school ... reduce the possibilities of standardised education provision and risk fragmentation.

However, the equity costs of plural forms of provision remain a matter of concern. Pluralism, both within private and public systems of education, and diversity of types of school (formal, non-formal, alternative) and types of providers (community, NGO, for-profit, public-private partnerships) all reduce the possibilities of standardised education provision and increase the risk of fragmentation. This is particularly the case in South Asia. For example, in India even the state school system is internally fragmented, composed of formal schools, alternative schools for excluded communities, and transitional and bridge schools for out-of-school children, particularly girls. On the one hand, these initiatives can be lauded as an attempt to introduce flexible measures to suit populations with diverse needs and constraints. But on the other hand, their quality

... the investment inequities between those children who can access reasonable schools and those whose access to schooling is restricted to non-formal models remain a matter of concern.

varies and they can become alternatives to quality formal schooling, doing little to provide meaningful alternatives and opportunities for children. For instance, it is argued that the rapid increase in girls' schooling can be attributed to the policy focus on alternative schools and forms of transitional schooling, such as bridge schools and residential camps, which are meant to be temporary measures aimed at integrating out-of-school girls into formal schools. Little is known about the impact of participation in these schools, not only about girls' learning and empowerment, but also whether they go on to complete formal schooling (Ramachandran, 2004).

The impact of pluralism on qualifications and their value in the labour market gives rise to one set of equity questions; another pertains to the quality of these forms of schooling and the investment made by the state, particularly in the realisation of the rights of the poorest children. The drive to enrol more children is resulting in the creation of different types of schools that reach the poorest children, including bridge schools that offer short-term courses to enable out-of-school children to catch up; non-formal or alternative education centres, which typically have shorter hours and less formal curricula; and 'education guarantee' schools run by para-teachers. This increase in provision has depended on reducing the unit costs of schooling. This has partly been achieved by hiring teachers outside the formal system on contract payments. So the investment inequities between children who can access reasonable schools and those whose access to schooling is restricted to non-formal models remain a matter of concern. Studies of the outcomes of such fragmented forms of educational provision – both in terms of access and quality – are typically small scale and controversial (see, for example, Leclercq, 2003).

There are no simplistic correlations between private schooling and good quality. Bennell (2003) notes that the overall quality of schooling in South Asia, regardless of ownership, is poor. Bray (1998) reviews studies of different Asian countries and finds that the evidence on quality differentials between private and public schools is inconclusive in most countries. While the continuing rise of private provision begs clear policy responses from South Asian governments, there is still a need for assessments of the relative quality, efficiency and equity merits of different kinds of non-state provision compared with government provision. Given the size of the share of the state in providing elementary schooling, the role played by the private sector is unlikely to reduce the need for effective reforms of educational financing and management.

For-profit non-state providers are typically more interested in providing schooling that is attractive to parents and children, and hence lucrative. Where demand for female schooling is low, for-profit providers are unlikely to be sufficiently motivated to function in ways that might encourage girls to attend school (Jha and Subrahmanian, 2006). In Pakistan, girls are more likely to be enrolled in public schools because private schools are typically mixed or boys-only (Sathar *et al.*, 2003).

While it could be argued that the spread of for-profit non-state schools is hard to contain in an era of globalisation where demands for specialist and varied forms of education are increasing, there remains a strong role for the state in providing cost-free education as part of a 'rights' framework, where the state assumes the obligation to ensure that every child is in school. For-profit schools are likely to respond to very particular types of demand, without any obligation to ensure equity in relation to the wider society in which they operate. Managing the spread of such schools with respect to wider social equity and acknowledging the right to quality education of all children is, however, a state obligation. It is important that governments ensure that public schools are well resourced and provide quality education, and that they regulate the spread of non-state providers and ensure that they support the EFA mandate in their practices, particularly with respect to quality and equity.

Box 4.9 The Impact of Mother-tongue Education

The intimate connections between schooling and home life are often underplayed when schools are being established as part of modernisation, nation-building and unification processes. These have usually meant the imposition of a dominant language throughout the education system in order to create a national identity and minimise linguistic differences between various ethnic groups. Most modern education systems focus on integrating students into a shrinking world and enabling them to participate in the global economy. This is also demonstrated by the increasing demand for English language instruction in schools in Anglophone countries.

But as recent research shows, mother-tongue education can be essential for building the confidence of children from disadvantaged groups or minorities who may feel marginalised if they are unable to communicate with other children or cannot learn easily. Mother-tongue education also meets parental concerns about the appropriateness of schooling, particularly for girls.

Studies in Guinea-Bissau, Niger and Mozambique have found that girls benefit enormously from bilingual schools, with greater enrolment, less repetition and lower drop-out rates than girls who study in a dominant language. Under-lying these findings is the greater confidence of parents in educational outcomes when daughters attend schools that communicate in a familiar language and their ability to participate more in school decision-making. Male teachers from the same linguistic or cultural communities as their students were more protective of their female students and had closer ties with students' families (Benson, 2005).

Kane (2004) reviewed studies from different countries and found that not only is mother-tongue education an issue relevant to the cultural rights of diverse groups, but the cognitive development of children may be positively affected if their learning is first carried out in their mother tongue: *'Research indicates that children need at least 12 years to learn their first language, that progress in the mother tongue is crucial to cognitive development and that children do not learn second languages any more easily than adults or older children'*. However, the difficulties of bilingual teaching in terms of both financial and human resources are also noted. Finding and training bilingual teachers and developing bilingual teaching materials can be very challenging for countries still in the process of ensuring universal enrolment.

Re-entry policies

Pregnancy and early marriage are a major impediment to girls' completion of elementary schooling. In some countries, where early pregnancy is a significant factor causing girls to drop out, advocacy has led to the formulation of re-entry policies for girls once they have had their babies. This has replaced an earlier approach (still in place in many countries) that excluded girls from school once they became pregnant.

However, re-entry policies that do not work with communities, parents and girls to assess the underlying causes of pregnancy do little to challenge the stigma attached to young unmarried mothers. Hence, re-entry policies may remain ineffective, with little impact on the learning opportunities offered to girls. Lack of counselling and sex education in schools exacerbates the problem, as young women receive little information about negotiating relationships, understanding the consequences of an unwanted pregnancy or how to care for a young child while studying. Peer group support may not be adequately encouraged. Dunne and Leach (2005) found that in Botswana and Ghana, two countries that have re-entry policies, teachers are reluctant to implement them and returning girls face an intimidating environment. Where schoolboys have fathered children, little attention is paid to encouraging them to support mothers and babies – they may be totally excluded, as in Botswana, or their potential role may be overlooked.

Re-entry policies offer a striking example of the overlap between society and school, where regardless of the reasons why a girl has become pregnant and of the relationship that has resulted in pregnancy, schools remain responsible under the commitment to universal education for ensuring minimum disruption of the girl's school career. The more schools work with parents and communities to strengthen that compact and ensure that girls do not drop out, the more likely is it that the reasons why girls become pregnant can be addressed.

Female teachers

Improving the gender balance among teachers is likely to yield significant results in the promotion of gender parity (Herz and Sperling, 2004). Evidence for sub-Saharan Africa shows that countries with roughly equal proportions of male and female

Improving the gender balance among teachers is likely to yield significant results in the promotion of gender parity.

... the vicious cycle of low gender parity leading to insufficient qualified young women teachers requires urgent policy attention.

primary teachers also have approximate equality in primary intakes (UNESCO, 2003: 60). As UNESCO's report notes, cause and effect are hard to unravel and it is not easy to see how the two are correlated – the number of women teachers could be the effect of greater gender parity in education, rather than being the cause of it; but the report concludes that the relationship is robust.

Female teachers are an important reminder to communities, parents and female pupils that education for women can open up new possibilities. Teaching is seen as a profession compatible with appropriate gender roles even in conservative settings, and female teachers can offer role models to young girls. It is striking that most women who become teachers do so because their families see teaching as an 'appropriate' profession for women, as the work involves children, allows regular vacations, does not involve much investment in training and is seen to be relatively easy in terms of the time and effort involved. Yet, for the very same reasons – the accommodation of women's dual responsibilities as home-makers and earners – women teachers are highly constrained in the effective fulfilment of their professional roles. They face restrictions in moving to take up teaching jobs in different areas, particularly away from urban centres, as the husband is often seen as the primary wage earner and determines where the woman works. Even when women work hard, they shy away from taking on responsibilities (and equally from getting credit) for what they do. Concerns about security in more remote areas deter single women teachers from moving to a new area.

Despite the fact that they are recognised as key actors in universalising girls' education, women teachers' needs and interests are rarely addressed. However, the vicious cycle of low gender parity leading to insufficient qualified young women teachers requires urgent policy attention. Without distributing available female teachers across regions, including more disadvantaged ones, patterns of female teacher deployment are likely to be uneven, exacerbating the variations in progress towards gender parity. In order to counter this problem, attention needs to be paid to the conditions of work, the provision of safe housing and the establishment of a system which recognises the degrees of hardship entailed in a posting with commensurate compensation.

Conclusion

Intersections between supply and demand need to be better understood, as it cannot be assumed that supply follows demand: instead, it must precede it and shape it in ways that are appropriate to the achievement of development policy goals. Parental decisions are influenced by community norms on appropriate gender roles and behaviours, but they are also increasingly influenced by perceptions of quality and the outcomes associated with schools. Parental decisions to educate girls may well be influenced by local norms regarding the appropriate age of marriage and the specific economic and other considerations that circumscribe the family's choices.

The rising demand for female schooling is evident in rapid rates of enrolment; the fact that schools are unable to retain pupils, as shown by high drop-out rates, indicates that the supply of good schooling is insufficient to meet new demand. Supply-side factors, including the lack of good quality, safe and accessible post-primary schools are likely to confirm the decision to drop out; conversely, the availability of good quality, safe and accessible schools may well challenge this decision and help break intergenerational cycles of educational deprivation.

Similarly, as discussed above, where parents are willing to make the tentative trade-off between investing in girls' education at the risk of exposing them to new non-traditional influences, these spaces offer opportunities to promote new ideas and ways of thinking about gender equality. In this regard the quality of teacher training is critical.

5. Policies and Programmes for Promoting Gender-equitable Schooling

The analysis so far has raised many issues regarding the complex social constructions that give rise to inequalities between women and men, and girls and boys, in many spheres of human and social life, including schooling and education. These complexities indicate the important role that schools can play in addressing a range of inequalities faced by children in order to improve their chances and opportunities in adulthood. Breaking intergenerational transfers of poverty and inequality requires investment in children's education today. However, the quality of schooling interventions matters, as does the ability of policies and programmes to locate schooling and the school within a wider set of socio-economic and political issues. Narrow sectoral approaches to education are failing to reach groups that are excluded on account of their social identity, geography or personal circumstances, and are failing to keep students at school.

Figure 5.1 attempts to capture this complexity in a simple diagram, building on the analysis presented in earlier chapters. The school is one of many institutions that impacts on a child's life. Others include the household, community, labour market and policy-making organisations of government that determine the allocation of resources and the policies through which the rights of the child can be realised in the public domain. Based on the analysis in the preceding chapters, the diagram maps complementary actions that could have an impact on the female child's ability to access education and progress through primary and secondary school, and beyond.

As the figure shows, policy actions need to simultaneously target a range of institutional sites that impinge on the female learner's ability to access education:

Households: Poverty and economic security are major factors determining access to schooling. Actions need to include the protection of vulnerable households against economic risk and

Figure 5.1 Policy Actions for a Multi-sited Approach to Education

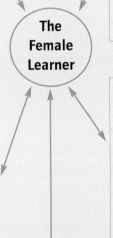

Households

- Livelihood security
- Social protection against economic risk
- Demand-side financing
- Creche or childcare support
- Overall improvements in availability of quality health, fuel, water and food security

Communities

- Inclusive community involvement in school governance
- Involvement in tracking out of school children and addressing their constraints
- Deliberation and discussion on reasons why girls discontinue schooling
- Awareness of and support for legal rights of women and girls

The Female Learner

State

- Equitable distribution of resources and infrastructure to reduce geographical and demographic bias in spread of quality services
- Adequate financial allocation to education to ensure subsidies are directed at reducing costs to the poor to the extent possible
- Improved management systems to increase locally responsive planning and flexible approaches
- Accountability systems in place to identify
- Regulation of plural providers to ensure equity
- Monitoring of progress through periodic gender-disaggregated and qualitative tracking of baseline data

Labour markets

- Vocational skills development, linking education to labour market
- Non-discriminatory recruitment and remuneration policies
- Supportive actions for elimination of child labour through payment of minimum wage and decent work conditions for adult workers

Schools

- Gender sensitive learning environments, including curriculum
- Accessible infrastructure to ensure full participation of disabled children
- Clean toilets and water supply
- Development of skills and capacities of every individual learner
- Psychosocial support for the emotional development of every learner
- Quality non-discriminatory teaching
- Complementary interventions such as school feeding, health
- Protection of learners from bodily harm and abuse
- Linkages between tiers of schooling to ensure smooth transition
- Encouragement of parental or guardian involvement in school management
- Continuous engagement with wider community within which school is located to ensure all children are in school regardless of social group, ability
- Simplified feedback mechanisms between schools and education administration bodies

vulnerability, and overall improvements in access to basic services, including health and nutrition, food security, water and domestic energy sources, and the right to decent work.

Communities: Actions should include the building of social norms that uphold the legal rights of a child to attend and complete school, delay their age of marriage, and be safe and protected from physical risks, including sexual abuse and unwanted early pregnancy.

Schools: Actions should focus on building gender-sensitive learning environments (including the curriculum) that develop the skills and capacities of every pupil. Investment in improving the quality of teaching, supportive programmes such as school feeding schemes and psycho-social care for each child, and rigorous standards to protect the safety of every child from abuse are also important.

Labour markets: The development of non-discriminatory opportunities for women and men, linkages with the education sector to promote the development of non-traditional vocational skills and support for efforts to eliminate child labour through ensuring that adult workers are paid at least the minimum wage and have decent conditions of work, are all actions that can strengthen education through creating incentives.

The state: The state plays a critical role in ensuring that all these actions are implemented. The policy environment must be improved to ensure that the state is responsive to the needs of diverse groups of children, sensitive to context and committed to ensuring that every child attends school. This implies reduced costs of schooling, improved management structures to allow locally relevant services to develop, improved accountability to ensure action when services are inaccessible, teachers are absent or the quality of teaching poor, and a system which develops 'backward and forward linkages' (Ramachandran, 2004) between different tiers of education, and among home, community and school.

While we have presented an exhaustive range of complementary actions, the success of educational reform depends on wider improvements in other areas and institutions; progress has to be made on all fronts, rather than sequentially, as was argued in Chapter 1.

... gender inequalities in education intersect with other forms of inequality and deprivation.

Lessons from Experience

Many reports and studies have reviewed international experience and 'best practice' in relation to strategies that 'work' for girls' education. These studies include a global review of evidence (Herz and Sperling, 2004), a review of experience in sub-Saharan Africa (Kane, 2004) and reports on the South Asian experience (UNICEF, 2003; Commonwealth Secretariat, 2005).

These studies provide useful summaries of strategies that have succeeded in boosting school participation, the main lessons of which are captured below.

Strategies that appear to have a positive impact

In a comprehensive review of strategies for promoting girls' education in sub-Saharan Africa, Kane (2004) draws on project documents, evaluation studies, national data, research studies, and practitioner and donor experiences and advocacy to identify evidence for the effectiveness of strategies. Based on this review, Kane makes the following observations about strategies that work:

Cross-sectoral interventions that go beyond a focus on schooling-related inputs to address inter-related sources of constraint. As has been argued above, gender inequalities in education intersect with other forms of inequality and deprivation. This suggests that narrow sectoral approaches will yield only limited results. As Kane (2004) points out, this is a 'common sense' strategy based on considerable evidence which locates poor education access and completion in the context of other socio-economic constraints.

Multiple interventions working within a flexible package. Addressing the multiple constraints on both demand and supply requires a well-conceived package of services with coordination between different service providers within and outside government. Large-scale sector-wide approaches offer possibilities for such coordinated efforts, linking financing to provision gaps based on baseline data and analytical studies of the causes of non-attendance at school. Kane also points out that many interventions that work for girls benefit all children. Gender-neutral interventions can, therefore, have an impact on girls, as long as they are tracked and monitored through a gender-disaggregated approach.

Ensuring that educational interventions are responsive and localised. This can make a critical difference, given the diversity of social groups and geographical terrains within countries. Examples include: bilingual programmes; recruiting local teachers and more female teachers; and creating alternative programmes that address the needs of diverse groups. Alternative programmes are a popular policy response to the challenge of achieving universal education. Alternative schools can be set up quickly as they employ teachers with fewer qualifications than formal schools, can by-pass delays in the recruitment and posting of teachers that are typical of larger centralised systems and avoid the complications of complex tendering processes in the building of schools. Though they are often most closely associated with innovation and rapid increases in enrolment, the qualitative and quantitative impacts of these programmes have not been sufficiently measured to enable broad conclusions to be drawn about their efficacy.

Meaningful community involvement. This is a critical factor in the success of programmes, as long as participation of all members of a given community is elicited and their views taken into account. Although community participation is a recognised component of many development programmes, in reality participation is often limited to local elites and to those who can exercise choice in relation to their children's schooling and other issues. Community participation has also been 'extractive', through the use of community resources such as labour and funds for furthering national government programmes, without having a commensurate share in decision-making (Rose, 2003). Thus extra efforts must be made to ensure that community participation is 'meaningful', involving sensitivity about the location, timing and methodology of meetings, and making sure that all opinions are voiced.

The process of involving communities requires an understanding of the ways in which communities 'think' about issues relating to gender and other social relations; the value of education in terms of their specific occupational and other strategies; and the kinds of services likely to be most attractive to them. Meanings attributed to education, to marriage and to

Alternative programmes are a popular policy response to the challenge of achieving universal education.

women's and men's roles in society are all important as entry points for programmes and communities to work together.

Making education accessible. Addressing costs and reducing the distance which children have to travel to school are well-established strategies with proven impacts and require little further discussion. Addressing costs includes both efforts to reduce the direct costs (fees) and indirect costs (uniforms, textbooks and other inputs) of schooling through increasing financial allocations and subsidies for the education sector. Demand-side financing policies, such as regular conditional cash transfers and scholarships and stipends for learners can also help to address the opportunity costs of schooling.

> ### Box 5.1 'Non-negotiables' for Success
>
> Kane's (2004) review suggests a range of factors that are likely to cause a project or programme to fail. These suggest, in turn, a range of non-negotiables that must inform any project or programme for girls' education:
>
> - Attention to the full range of economic costs to families and communities;
>
> - Attention to the 'cultural' costs perceived by communities to arise from educating girls at the expense of traditions such as early marriage;
>
> - Adaptation of strategies that have worked elsewhere;
>
> - Well-designed projects, where cycles of analysis, design and planning, implementation, monitoring and redesign are executed in a sequence of learning and improvement, with a supporting management structure;
>
> - Fostering meaningful community participation and involvement.

Below we summarise a full range of complementary education strategies that can make a significant difference to the schooling experiences of all children, and girls in particular, drawing on the numerous reviews of international experience undertaken or supported by international development agencies in recent years.

Table 5.1 Complementary Strategies through the Schooling Cycle

Goal	Strategies
Being able to enrol in school	Having an elementary school nearby
	Fee-free and cost-free elementary schooling (i.e. no direct fees or indirect costs)
	Demand-side financing targeted at vulnerable groups/children for whom the opportunity costs of education are high
	Residential schools for children of migrant labourers
	Mobile schools for mobile or remote populations
	Bridge courses or transitional education centres for older out-of-school children, with linkages established to formal schools
	Early childhood education programmes to ensure school preparedness and nutritional development, and improve health status
Being able to stay in school all day	Clean toilets and safe water supply
	School feeding programmes
	Safety in school with teachers responsible for ensuring that girls leave school safely with and responsible adult or with peers
	Community level crèche/childcare) facilities for younger children
	School calendar sensitive to local festivals, seasonal labour and weather patterns
Being able to stay in school, learn and progress through the elementary schooling cycle	Quality teaching/regular teacher attendance
	Remedial education within the school for children falling behind
	Availability of female teachers
	Regular income support for poorest households
	Free/subsidised textbooks, uniforms, stationery, targeted as appropriate
	Parental involvement in child's progress and encouragement to parents to continue to educate their children
	School health programmes to provide periodic check-ups
	Bilingual teaching where relevant
	Protective measures to ensure safety, dignity and self-esteem of learners with particular emphasis on tackling gender-based violence
	Peer support networks in contexts of health crises, such as HIV/AIDS, and also to help girls develop strategies to counter parental pressure to drop out or marry
	Adult women forums to encourage their leadership to champion the cause of female education
	Attention to the conditions of work for teachers, improvements in performance management and training
Being able to complete schooling	Encouragement to parents/guardians of girls to participate in exams
	Re-entry policies for pregnant girls
Being able to complete transition into the next stage of schooling	Availability of secondary schools in the vicinity
	Residential schools or facilities for girls
	Safe and affordable transportation to secondary schools
	Proactive measures to encourage girls to attend secondary schools, including single-sex schools, stipends and scholarships

Cash transfers are increasingly being used as a policy tool to complement supply-side interventions ...

Strategies for state action that can make a difference

As Table 5.1 shows, there are a range of strategies and actions that can be taken to ensure that all children's experience of school is a worthwhile private and public investment. In this handbook we elaborate on three strategies that can be undertaken by states and can make a critical difference to the educational prospects of girl learners in particular. These strategies are selected as examples of very different entry points to addressing the various constraints to female schooling.

They are:

- Demand-side financing through conditional cash transfers, addressing constraints arising from household poverty and vulnerability;

- Empowering adult women and building cadres of female workers and teachers, thereby addressing gender-equitable management through the creation of role models and champions of change, which can in turn transform community and household norms and values;

- Dealing with sexual harassment and protecting female learners against violence, thereby addressing fundamental gender ideologies that prevent girls from entering public spaces without fear, and help create norms of gender equality between boys and girls at an early age.

1 Demand-side financing through conditional cash transfers

Cash transfers are increasingly being used as a policy tool to complement supply-side interventions aimed at increasing the access of the poor and disadvantaged to essential social services. Defined as *'the provision of assistance in the form of cash to the poor or to those who face a probable risk, in the absence of the transfer, of falling into poverty'* (Tabor, 2002), cash transfers are seen as valuable policy measures to address human poverty. Based on the recognition that both supply- and demand-side factors constrain the access of poor and excluded groups and individuals to essential health and education services, cash transfers are being used in several countries to bolster demand for and utilisation of services by providing regular income supplements that can be used to cover the direct and/or opportunity costs of access.

Conditional cash transfers (CCTs), which focus household expenditures on particular essential services, in addition to providing income supplements, are a policy tool which can be used to address poverty-related constraints and improve the human capital of the poor. In particular, conditional cash transfers emphasise the importance of behaviour change, incentivising households to make specific investments that address poverty-induced constraints to developing human capital and thereby yield human capital gains. Where parents are given cash to make investments in their children's welfare, it is important to ensure that the additional income is spent in a way that guarantees benefits to the child. Conditions must be put in place which focus household expenditure on child well-being in return for income supplements which smooth household incomes.

The popularity of cash transfer schemes can be attributed to several factors. They offer greater flexibility to poor households in determining the use of their income than in-kind demand-side transfers (such as free uniforms or free textbooks), based on the recognition that households may have varying reasons for not taking up existing services that specific in-kind inputs may not address. In other words, while in-kind transfers may guarantee that households consume essential goods and services, the '*effectiveness and desirability of imposing a specific kind of consumption on the poor*' is questioned (Barrientos and DeJong, 2004).

Further, regular cash transfers may help households smooth over fluctuations in income and consumption, and other shocks that can disrupt access to services, and thereby reduce the vulnerability of poor households to unanticipated shocks, such as poor health, bereavement, loss of employment and seasonal variations. Children are often used to help households cope with risk (de Janvry *et al.*, 2004). For example, drought or seasonal variations in income relating to the agricultural cycle can result in disruptions to children's education with potential consequences for their attendance, learning and completion of schooling. Even though publicly provided education is 'fee free' in India, there remain significant costs which households must bear in relation to schooling (Tilak, 1996). Income fluctuations may prevent a household from being able to finance these additional and often hidden costs.

Conditional cash transfers ... are a policy tool which can be used to address poverty-related constraints and improve the human capital of the poor.

CCT programmes in various countries have shown positive impacts relating to child health and education indicators, and in many cases have also had a redistributive impact on incomes and reduced poverty levels.

Finally, cash transfers are relatively simple to administer and manage, as they are fiscally predictable in that expenditure can be forecast once the criteria and basis for targeting have been established. They also limit the involvement of service providers compared with in-kind transfer schemes.

The growing popularity of cash transfer schemes is evident in the increasing number of countries that have introduced them; they are particularly aimed at initiating short-term changes in household investment in children, with long-term implications for improvements in child well-being. Table 5.2 presents information on the best-known examples of such schemes.

As the table shows, many conditional cash transfer schemes that are aimed at benefiting children could be more accurately termed 'conditioned transfers for education'. Schemes in Mexico, Brazil, Bangladesh and elsewhere (Morley, 2004) have focused on providing cash transfers to households in return for school attendance. In these programmes poverty is defined as deprivation of essential human capabilities. In addition to education-related conditionalities that are monitored at school level, some of these schemes also include health-related conditionalities and supplement demand-side subsidies with direct transfers to schools and hospitals to improve the quality of services. These programmes are widely credited with significant improvements in enrolment, attendance and completion of schooling, particularly for girls.

Many cash transfer programmes have expanded the focus from education and health to wider multi-dimensional concerns relating to poverty. They seek to shield the poor (and especially the most vulnerable among the poor) from income shocks, such as in South Africa and the 'transition economies' of Central Asia and Eastern Europe, or they seek to address a wide range of issues that combine to exacerbate chronic poverty, such as Chile Solidario.

CCT programmes in various countries have had positive impacts on child health and education indicators, and in many cases have also had a redistributive impact on incomes and reduced poverty levels. While it is too early to measure the effect on long-term and intergenerational poverty, there has been positive impacts on variables targeted under the different schemes (Barrientos and DeJong, 2004). Collateral benefits can also result, such as greater participation of women in social development programmes, increased civil registration and increased access to financial systems such as banks for poor people (Britto, 2005).

Box 5.2 Some Lessons Learned from Cash Transfer Programmes Worldwide

- Cash transfers benefit children even when they are targeted at other household members, and are thus appropriate policy tools for empowering vulnerable household members and addressing the distribution of resources within the household.

- Cash transfers alone may not be effective – they need to be complemented by the provision of basic services to the poor. Hence, continued increases in spending on the supply of services are necessary, together with demand-side payments (Barrientos and DeJong, 2004).

- It is important to ensure 'vertical' efficiency in reaching the poor (i.e. reducing leakage to those who are better off) as well as 'horizontal' efficiency (i.e. reaching all poor people).

- Early childhood is a key stage for interventions aimed at improving child well-being, particularly making linkages between health, nutritional status and education.

- Targeting payments to mothers yields considerably greater benefits for girl children, and is the best way of ensuring that money is spent on nutrition and other consumption expenditure for children (Barrientos and DeJong, 2004; Tietjen, 2003).

- Baseline data, and regular monitoring and evaluation are essential for improving the efficiency of programmes.

Table 5.2   Features of Successful CCT Programmes

Programme and Aim	Features	Targeting and Conditions	Coverage and Cost	Impacts
Progresa, Mexico *Support for poor households with children in small rural communities*	Payment of US$12.5 household consumption subsidy per household per month *Plus* school subsidy of between US$8 and US$30.5 per child of school-going age per month, depending on the school grade *Plus* annual subsidy of between US$15.5 and US$20.5 per child to cover school materials Overall benefit capped at US$75 per household	Two-stage targeting: first, geographical to cover poorer areas and communities based on population and services coverage; second, poorer households based on an index of socio-economic indicators (i.e. means-testing) Conditions: 85 per cent attendance at school; mothers and infants regularly attending primary healthcare examinations and parenting sessions	Coverage: 2.6 million households in 2002 . (approx. 40 per cent of rural households)	• Reduced poverty gap by 36% • Reduced child stunting • Reduced adult and childhood illness • Increased school enrolments, particularly among girls and at secondary school
ProgramaBolsa Escola, Brazil *Reduce child labour and improve school enrolment*	Cash supplements to households with an income lower than US$90 per month		US$5–15 to households with children aged 6–15 years 8.2 million children in 5 million households reached Cost: 0.7 per cent of total public spending, 2.5 per cent of government spending on education (2001)	• Reduction in child labour • Rise in school enrolments and attainments
Chile Solidario, Chile *Provide comprehensive and sustained support to extremely poor households*	Households assigned social worker for first 24 months who arranges support relating to health, education, household dynamics, work, income and housing, based on a contract signed with the household.		113,116 households living in extreme poverty, to be expanded to over 250,000 households in 2005	

Programme and Aim	Features	Targeting and Conditions	Coverage and Cost	Impacts
Chile Solidario, Chile (*continued*)	Services tailored to the needs of the household.			
Bangladesh Primary Education Stipend Programme (2002 onwards) *Increase education participation of primary school-aged children from poor households*	Cash assistance to targeted poor households in all rural areas whose children (40 per cent of all pupils) are enrolled in eligible primary schools (government registered, non-government, community schools, satellite schools, approved NGO schools, recognised Ebtedayee Madrassahs) – with a minimum of 100 pupils	40 per cent of all pupils enrolled in grades 1–5 from the poorest house-holds. Identification done by SMCs with assistance from head-teachers approved by Upazilla Primary Education Officer Poor children selected: – from distressed female-headed households – children of day labourers – children of insolvent artisans/mechanics – from landless families – children of share-croppers Questions raised about the problems of targeting criteria used (eligible schools nominate 40 per cent of their poorest students) Conditions: selected pupils must maintain 85 per cent monthly attendance and attain a minimum of 50 per cent marks on annual exam administered for each grade. Participating schools must demonstrate at least 60 per cent pupil attendance; 10 per cent of its grade 5 pupils must sit for the primary school scholarship exam.	Coverage: Rural areas – 65,000 schools and 5.5 million students at an estimated cost of approx. $600 million To be expanded in 2004 to urban areas but no information Households of qualifying pupils receive 100 taka per month per pupil, and 125 taka per month for more than one pupil	No studies as yet, but design based on lessons learned from earlier PES (smaller scale) and Food for Education. Impacts associated with these earlier programmes shows positive impact on school enrolments

Table 5.2 (continued)

Programme and Aim	Features	Targeting and Conditions	Coverage and Cost	Impacts
Female Secondary School Stipend Programme, Bangladesh *Short-term objectives:* • *to achieve an increase in girls enrolment in grades VI–X* • *to assist female students to pass their SSC examinations so that they can participate in economic activities* • *to curb early marriage by extending the length of time girls remain in school* *Long-term objectives:* • *to increase the number of educated women capable of participating in the economic and social development of Bangladesh* • *to increase the social status of women, particularly at community level and reduce gender gap* • *to reduce population growth by curbing early marriage*	Stipends are paid to families and are subject to annual performance measurement according to the qualification criteria. Schools are given additional awards (outside the stipend programme), e.g. for furniture and equipment, including computers, based on exam pass rates	The Female Stipend Programme provides stipends and tuition waivers to girls residing in all non-municipal areas attending grades VI–X. The stipend varies from 25 to 60 taka per month (with tuition costs of 10–5 taka per month paid directly to the school). Qualification criteria are: • a minimum 75 per cent attendance rate • a minimum 45 per cent in annual school exams • girls remain unmarried up to sitting for the SSC exam or turning 18		

Source: Morley (2004); Tietjen (2003); Barrientos and DeJong (2004)

2 Empowering adult women

As argued in earlier chapters, adult women hold a strategic key to processes of change. Social transformations that allow them to play an active role in public decision-making will have a positive impact on young girls in terms of expanding their awareness of the possibilities for their own futures. Working with adult women involves two important elements: first, the creation of informal spaces and associations where women can discuss issues that are of importance to them and devise collective strategies or gain peer support for changes they would like to make; second, the establishment of linkages between informal associations and formal community decision-making organisations, such as user committees and parent-teacher bodies. Merely reserving places for women on formal committees has little impact on their ability to participate freely – many studies have shown how these spaces are often coopted by the powerful husbands of women members, and that women are often reserved and inhibited in the presence of more confident, articulate and often better educated men. Helping women to become more assertive and articulate requires the creation of spaces for women to meet and work through their personal experiences and identify their own perspectives.

The same strategies that are used to empower adult women can also be used to empower female teachers, as the discussion below elaborates, particularly where efforts are being made to improve the gender balance in the teaching profession in a short time-frame. NGO interventions in India and other parts of South Asia provide examples of innovative ways in which adult women can be involved in supporting girls' education and ways in which women teachers can be supported to play a more critical role in education.

Experience from India

Experience from India has shown many different ways in which women's collective action can have a positive impact on the development of women's capabilities, as well as contribute to changes in the intergenerational reproduction of values and norms relating to gender equality (Jain, 2004; Ramachandran, 2003; 2004). Many innovative programmes for women's empowerment have been set in motion, notably through education programmes.

... adult women hold a strategic key to processes of change. Social transformations that allow them to play an active role in public decision-making will have a positive impact on young girls in terms of expanding their awareness of the possibilities for their own futures.

Investing in adult women is one of the key interventions that can have a significant and meaningful impact on female education.

A significant feature of innovative programmes that have made an impact on female education is their investment in cadres of women involved in different aspects of education – management, teaching, community mobilisation – and their emphasis on women's participation. Programmes such as **Lok Jumbish** and **Shiksha Karmi** in Rajasthan and **Mahila Samakhya** in several states of India have demonstrated the importance of building women's capacities and skills and giving them positions of responsibility in the sphere of education. Investing in adult women is one of the key interventions that can have a significant and meaningful impact on female education. This involves, however, substantial investment in processes of confidence building and awareness-raising to ensure that women feel equipped to fulfil new roles and responsibilities. Support for women cadres who may need to defend processes of change that are otherwise resisted by their communities, such as delaying the age of marriage of girls, is also critical.

The Shiksha Karmi project in Rajasthan focused on training women as education workers, or *shikshakarmis*, to promote awareness and encourage the enrolment of girls. Low levels of literacy, particularly female literacy, in Rajasthan mean that it is often nearly impossible to find qualified women to work as teachers in the formal education system. Because of the conservative nature of feudal Rajasthani society, women are often prevented from coming forward to participate in government programmes and in the education sector. The project appointed *Mahila shikshakarmis*, or women teachers, through an intensive outreach and training programme. In order to find women willing to become involved in the face of parental and community resistance, the project focused on daughters-in-law of a village, as they were likely to remain within the community. The project thus needed to invest in the confidence and skills of young women to enable them to overturn conventional domestic expectations and play a public role. However, the demands of this new role, which included travelling for training and being away from home, generated resistance from families and communities. Supportive supplementary interventions included setting up training centres for women (*Mahila Prasikshan Kendras*) to develop new skills and capacities for women teachers.

A supportive cadre of women helpers was also developed to escort young girls to school and back, and provide childcare during school hours so as to free up the labour of school-age girls who would otherwise have to look after their younger siblings. At state level, a further cadre of women served as a women's task force, which provided dedicated support to the women workers at field level.

These multiple layers of women cadres are a major step towards ensuring that more women actively participate in educational processes. They contribute in three important ways: empowering adult women and demonstrating their potential in playing an active public role; ensuring that women help motivate younger girls to go to school and perceive themselves as agents of change; and creating a momentum within the education system for the inclusion of women as part of the process of change.

Another programme, Lok Jumbish, also views women as critical agents in education management and delivery, and attempts to include women as equal participants at all levels of decision-making. Field functionaries and gender experts are brought together in a forum to discuss gender issues and advise project managers. Jain (2003: 19) notes that 'the assumption running through Lok Jumbish management is that shifts in gender attitudes have to be created and nurtured at all levels of the planned intervention'. Trained women work within a cluster of villages and provide support to women's groups in each village. The village groups promote girls' access to schooling and monitor the regularity of educational transactions, as well as provide inputs into education planning for out-of-school children. Lok Jumbish has also started a forum for women teachers, recognising the need for mutual support, a Women's Residential Institute for Training and Education (WRITE) to provide training and education for young women up to grade 8 and residential camps for adolescent girls to allow girls who have married young or been denied the opportunity for schooling to receive some formal education.

Lok Jumbish's interventions foreground the challenges faced by women and girls where school attendance comes up against ingrained prejudices and obstacles. Jain (2003) notes that girls' brothers were often the most resistant to their sisters' participation in educational camps, and often ridiculed them

... new issues arising from gender equality interventions are often not taken up ... because management capacities are incapable of coping with the complex nature of social change and the often unforeseen consequences of the interventions.

or were even physically violent. She also notes, importantly, that new issues arising from gender equality interventions are often not taken up, even within an innovative programme like Lok Jumbish, because management capacities are incapable of coping with the complex nature of social change and the often unforeseen consequences of the interventions. This emphasises the importance of sustained follow-up, flexibility and responsiveness, all of which are features that require radical changes to management structures, inimical as they are to the current hierarchical functioning of public service delivery systems.

Mahila Samakhya, set up as a programme operating within the Department of Education, has come closest to generating innovative pro-women strategies within the education system. While all major education programmes (the District Primary Education Programme and Sarva Shiksha Abhiyan) have incorporated Mahila Samakhya within their overall strategy, the programme is seen as having a distinct approach. Mahila Samakhya stands out among education interventions because of its explicit redefinition of education as a process of maximising potential through self-realisation. Thus its strategies for women's education include promoting self-confidence and self-esteem through intensive collective reflection processes; building the negotiation and articulation skills of poor women to enable them to deal with authority figures and structures within the home, community and state; enabling women to be aware about their bodies, their health and their rights; supporting women's livelihood strategies through developing vocational skills, credit and savings; and finally, promoting functional and legal literacy.

Mahila Samakhya puts into practice the understanding that education cannot be seen in isolation from the wider processes of society, livelihood and power. The recognition that education participation and outcomes rely on interlinkages with other capabilities and skills has led to an approach that allows women in each local context to collectively set priorities for their empowerment. Education may or may not be women's first priority – for example, in many programme locations, violence and bodily integrity have been identified as important precursors to enjoying full rights to education (Jain, 2003). Collective action also sees education as a process that is inbuilt in social relations, not distinct from it. Both these dimensions of the Mahila Samakhya approach are profound in terms of their departure from the conventional notion of education as a set of skills and credentials that develop individual capacities and bring individual returns.

Box 5.3 'Thinking out of the Box': NGO Strategies for Female Teachers in South Asia

Several NGOs in the South Asian region have demonstrated innovative strategies for placing women teachers and women managers at the heart of the process of change.

Some examples:

- For the Bangladesh Rural Advancement Committee (BRAC), Bangladesh, female teachers represent a revolution in Bangladeshi society. Female teachers reverse the stereotypical view of the male teacher or 'master'. BRAC teachers are locally recruited and often have only a few years of schooling. By recruiting women otherwise based in the home, BRAC has helped rural women find new respect within their societies. Women project staff are provided with bicycles and motorcycles to improve their mobility. The safety of women staff is paramount, and BRAC has guidelines for working conditions for all staff that deal with physical assault or harassment. BRAC allows women three days of desk work in every month and four months maternity leave with pay, and provides them with semi-furnished residential facilities.

- The Education Guarantee Scheme (EGS) in Madhya Pradesh, India, tackled the concern that the recruitment of local teachers with no professional qualifications may affect the quality of education provided by setting up a large-scale diploma certificate correspondence course in education for EGS teachers who have not received this training.

- A Pakistan NGO, the Society for the Advancement of Education (SAHE), also provides teachers with opportunities to improve their educational qualifications. By encouraging and recruiting large numbers of women teachers, SAHE has developed an environment in local communities where families that were initially reluctant to send their girls to teach in schools are now filing applications with the regional office.

- The Adhyapika Manch (Teacher's Forum) initiative of Lok Jumbish, an education programme in Rajasthan, India, evolved out of a realisation that women teachers had low rates of participation in teacher training programmes. Residential programmes were not suitable for women teachers with young children; the dominance of men as both participants and trainers in the training programme was intimidating to most women; family members resisted their participation; and women were reluctant to develop professional skills. The initiative therefore sought to work with women teachers to understand their constraints and inhibitions in a more holistic perspective, and to work with their families to mobilise support for them. It also tried to identify the facilities that women needed at the training centres. Through the forum, women teachers found collective solutions to what had hitherto been considered to be personal problems and developed a support structure that helped women stay in their jobs.

- Udaan, a project of the international NGO CARE in Uttar Pradesh, India, introduced a social learning curriculum that rested heavily on the ability and willingness of teachers to use the new approach to learning. As teachers themselves are products of a socialisation and education process that has hitherto neglected issues of equity, diversity and tolerance, getting teachers to discuss these issues required intensive teacher training. The process of curriculum development accompanied an intensive year-long training process, which involved making teachers conscious of unequal and differentiated practices in society, building their commitment to equity, developing the required skills and competence to undertake the desired activities, and raising their confidence about their capacity to deal with these issues with young children. Investing in teachers' capacities was a important first step to evolving the social curriculum for children.

Commonwealth Secretariat, 2005

3 Addressing sexual harassment and violence against girls

As noted earlier, there are few studies of sexual harassment and violence against girls at school, but those that have been carried out have exposed the endemic nature of physical and emotional violence in schools among peers, among teachers and among students and teachers. Taking action on these issues is critical for several reasons beyond the principal one of securing the rights of all individuals against abuse. First, for girls and boys, school is their first experience of cross-sex socialisation, and the experience of any form of violence or abuse will colour later relationships and institutional functioning. Second, if schools are to function as primary social institutions, they need to set and maintain standards of behaviour that can be upheld by other institutions and by children as they become adults. Setting these standards is also necessary if schools are to function as sites of education about HIV/AIDS – very often, prevalence of active sex discrimination and violence can run counter to HIV/AIDS prevention programmes.

However, as Leach *et al.* (2003a; 2003b) note, the lack of research into this issue and of examples of 'good practice' are a reflection of the lack of attention paid to violations of rights within the school environment. Even where legal protection is in place, as in South Africa, perpetrators are often acquitted or there are long delays in hearing cases. In the meantime a child's education can be severely disrupted. Teachers' unions often protect teachers charged with rape or abuse. Administrators and headteachers are often reluctant to report cases

... studies of sexual harassment and violence against girls at school ... have exposed the endemic nature of physical and emotional violence in schools among peers, among teachers and among students and teachers.

because of administration and media attention. Thus Leach *et al.* (2003a) conclude that education administrators and teachers often collude to divert attention from violence within the school, particularly sexual violence. Parents are also reluctant for attention to be paid to sexual abuse experienced by their daughters because of the 'shame' that is often attached to the experience.

Box 5.4 Defining Gender-based Violence in Schools

An important aspect of directing policy attention to a set of problems is defining the problem, so that its various aspects can be recognised and addressed. Gender-based violence in schools, whether between peers, between teachers, or between learners and teachers, can range from verbal to sexual abuse, and includes punishment by teachers. Violence or abuse in schools may involve:

- Rape

- Inappropriate teacher conduct – passing lewd remarks, writing love letters

- Threats or attempted coercion to have sex in return for better grades

- Corporal punishment

- Verbal abuse as a form of punishment

- Humiliation as a form of punishment – making learners stand or sit in awkward positions

- Bullying

While the overwhelming majority of violent incidents involve male perpetrators and female victims, bullying and gang wars take place between male peers. Female teachers may also use verbal abuse against pupils. Corporal punishment is often used by male teachers against male students. Boys may seek to punish girls if romantic overtures are made and then rejected.

Leach *et al.*, 2003a; 2003b

Manifestations of violence in schools have several underlying causes. Schools are social institutions and often reflect the wider asymmetries in power relations that are more widely prevalent in society. Authority is marked not just by gender, but by age, ethnicity, ability and other markers of social differentiation. Violence is often used as a marker of authority and to 'remind' learners of the power structures that they encounter in everyday life. Teachers also often use forms of violence and abuse to restate their authority in a classroom setting. Schools often allow teachers discretionary powers to assert their authority in the form of rewards and punishments, and transgressions often go unchecked. Teachers' own biases often come into play, particularly their assumptions about what constitutes gender-appropriate behaviour. Aggression displayed by boys in the classroom may thus be considered appropriate 'masculine' behaviour, and girls at the receiving end of teasing or humiliation may be expected to submit to such behaviour without challenge.

Teachers who engage in sexual relations with young students are in transgression of laws that criminalise sex with minors, but as noted above, the very authority that teachers exercise in the school may shield them from legal action. Making teachers accountable to communities, to parents and to learners is a critical step. Where national laws are weak, they need to be strengthened. Codes of conduct governing violence within schools need to be formulated, disseminated and discussed with parents. Redress mechanisms and grievance bodies need to be set up so that issues of violence can be taken up by learners and parents, and counselling can be provided to ensure that harmful effects are addressed.

Experience from South Africa

Gender-based violence in schools receives far too little attention in education policies and programmes, particularly in developing countries. However, experience in South Africa suggests strategies that can be put in place to counter sexual abuse in schools and ensure that children feel safe. These strategies are summarised below (based on Ramagoshi, 2005).

Legal framework: Strict disciplinary measures have been initiated since 2000 to address abuse against learners by educators, and immediate dismissal is the penalty, regardless of 'con-

Gender-based violence in schools receives far too little attention in education policies and programmes, particularly in developing countries.

sent' being argued or the pupil being from a different school.

Curriculum strengthening: The management of sexual abuse has been introduced into the *Curriculum 2005* policy within the 'Life Orientation/Life Skills Learning Area', through a focus on relationship between the sexes and discussion and analysis of relationships and values.

Creating spaces and forums to discuss safety and violence: The Department of Education's Culture of Learning and Teaching Campaign in 1998 had a creative arts initiative component, which aimed to provide learners with a non-threatening forum in which to discuss barriers to their learning, with particular emphasis on issues of safety, based on learners' priority concerns.

Development of management guidelines for school administration: A school-based module called *Managing Sexual Harassment and Gender-Based Violence* has been developed with education district officials, educators and schools in three provinces and is being disseminated nationwide. Developed through workshops, the module focuses on raising awareness about gender-based violence and provides institution-based policies and programmes to deal with it.

Other resources for school management and educators as well as for members of school governing bodies and members of the wider community include a workbook developed by the Department of Education and the South African Police Service in 2001 called *Signposts for Safe Schools*, which provides strategies to address violence in schools, focusing on the impact, authority and efficiency of school management and school services, as well as mobilisation strategies for young people.

Sexual harassment guidelines have also been recently developed and are being finalised by the Department of Education through an extensive process of consultation with stakeholders including teacher unions, student leadership, traditional and religious leaders, and civil society organisations. The aim is to assist school mangement teams in managing sexual harassment and dealing with reported cases.

Development of resources and guidelines on a range of gender issues: In addition to issues of violence, guidelines have been developed to deal with teenage pregnancy, based on inputs from pregnant teenage girls and girls participating in the Girls' Education Movement (GEM), which focuses on organising young women and men to promote leadership and equal partnerships. Gender resource pages are inserted monthly into a newsletter for teachers, linking curriculum policy to practice by developing model lessons. General resources in the form of a handbook on gender equity in education has also been made available to educators. Guidelines on drug abuse management have also been developed.

Focus on boys' empowerment: Recognising that gender-based violence cannot be tackled without involving boys as strategic partners and agents of change, workshops have been held on gender, masculinity, responsible sexuality and HIV/AIDS, and school-based programmes are being developed in this area.

The South African experience is particularly shaped by the widespread prevalence of violence. It is also aided, however, by a proactive reform movement, as well as an institutional structure that vests management leadership at the level of the individual school. This allows for school-specific issues to be tackled directly by school managers, who in turn are supported by the Department of Education through the development of guidelines, training and resources. The overall policy framework of the country encourages these developments through providing clear messages through policy and law.

... simultaneous efforts need to be made to provide cross-sectoral support to learners and their families, and also to improve the quality of schools and their management framework.

Conclusion

This chapter has mapped the range of interventions that are being tried out around the world to accelerate girls' education and reduce gender inequalities. As has been argued consistently, multiple strategies require simultaneous attention. Many governments focus on access as a first step policy concern. However, simultaneous efforts need to be made to provide cross-sectoral support to learners and their families, and also to improve the quality of schools and their management framework. The overall management structure of schools needs to be clarified; in many countries, schools are not given the central position that they deserve in the framework of education systems. They are treated as the outposts of the system, rather than the hub or centre. Investing in school governance and creating relationships of accountability among policy-makers, community members, learners and their guardians, and school management are important reforms that can strengthen local involvement in schooling within a pro-active policy environment.

6. Institutional Transformation and Gender Mainstreaming in Education

A gender analysis in the education sector would begin from a consideration of the ways in which boys and girls, men and women, participate differently in the education system. This would entail not only looking at enrolment at one specific time in the school system, but also completion issues, transfer rates to more advanced levels, various quality concerns, etc. Secondly, as part of a mainstreaming strategy, the gender analysis would seek to identify structure and processes – legislation, social and political institutions, cultural practices, learning and teaching institutions' practices, etc. – that can act to perpetuate girls' advantage. The purpose is to identify whether special steps are needed to enable women and girls to participate and benefit and which opportunities exist to reduce gender gaps. The outcome of this exercise would be education policies, programmes and projects which will serve both men and women and contribute to achieving more equal gender relations in the education sector at large.

OECD-DAC, 1999: 27–28

In order for the Platform for Action to be implemented, it will be necessary for Governments to establish or improve the effectiveness of national machineries for the advancement of women at the highest political level.

UN, 1995: para. 296

The EFA movement set goals for achieving gender parity that are still unmet in many countries, despite substantial progress. A factor explaining the lack of international outcry at the goals being missed is that perhaps the timelines were unrealistic and that steady progress shows that enough is being done. After all, as we have seen, bringing about gender equality within and through education requires locating the schooling process and the learner within the multiple relationships and institutions that together produce quality universal educational outcomes. Without work on these relationships through

While public policy action cannot resolve these societal questions, it can play a critical role in providing opportunities for such debate by being a catalyst for the exchange of new ideas.

systematic public action, sustainable changes in the gender equations in education will be hard to realise.

An underlying factor is the absence of definitional clarity on what gender *equality* in education means, as we have seen in Chapter 2. Definitions of equality underline the importance of societal debate and consensus on the shared value given to gender equality in a given setting. While public policy action cannot resolve these societal questions, it can play a critical role in providing opportunities for such debate by being a catalyst for the exchange of new ideas.

Institutionalising gender equality as a basic requirement of public policy is, therefore, necessary in order to enable public actors to engage in the creation of new modes of thinking and doing. A fundamental challenge in meeting the Education for All targets and the MDGs on gender equality and women's empowerment through education is how to ensure that policies move beyond their current focus on parity to the more challenging demands of equity and equality. Current policies have been successful in generating 'parity effects', but they are weak in creating opportunities for generating 'equality effects'. This is partly the consequence of weak policy and a lack of interest in the wider transformative struggles that the quest for equality signifies. Making transformation a discernable aspect of the public policy agenda is thus a challenge for national governments and the international agencies and civil society organisations that seek to influence them.

Why Gender Mainstreaming?

Gender mainstreaming is a critical strategy for ensuring that women's rights are addressed through development policy formulation and the planning and implementation processes, as these processes determine who the recipients of public resources are, the grounds on which they can claim entitlement, the preconditions and qualifications they are expected to have to receive the resources, and the benefits that the investments are likely to yield to the recipients and to state and society.

In the early years of concern about women's relative disadvantage in all spheres of life, including health, education and work, efforts were made to reach women within the home and in their conventional spheres of work without questioning why sex-based inequalities were prevalent the world over. The evolution of conceptual thinking on issues relating to the perceived and real differences between women and men, or differences based on 'gender', allowed the important question to be posed: why do women experience systematic inequalities relative to men and why are these differences found in diverse settings and contexts? The illumination of the social construction of norms and values that structure male and female identities, define socially appropriate behaviours and roles, and hence delineate the kinds of resources considered necessary for women and men, helped make apparent the dynamics of discrimination that have resulted in patterns of gender inequality being reproduced over time.

Box 6.1 **The Origins of Gender Mainstreaming**

Byrne *et al.* (1996: 8) note that: 'In 1962, the United Nations Commission on the Status of Women first identified the value of appointing national commissions on the status of women which were to make recommendations for improving the position of women in their respective countries'.

The UN definition of national machinery is 'a single body or complex organised system of bodies, often under different authorities, but recognised by the Government as the institution dealing with the promotion of the status of women' (ibid.). According to this view, national machinery is understood to be a transitional measure for accelerated action towards equal opportunities and the integration of women into public life. Byrne *et al.* note that the 'creation of state women's machineries (as well as similar structures in donor agencies and NGOs) raised expectations that women's needs would be addressed in development policy and planning. By 1985, 90 per cent of countries had established some form of national machinery for women, 50 per cent of which had been set up during the first Decade for Women (1975–1985).'

... bringing gender into the mainstream means making gender equality goals 'key decision-making criteria that are pursued from the centre, rather than the margins'.

Ensuring that development policies that affect the well-being of both men and women become sensitive to gender differences has been the focus of energetic women's movements across the world, which have extended concerns with gender inequality in the developed world to concerns with uneven development and gender inequality in developing countries. Coalitions of women's groups working across national boundaries combined with the more formal drive towards gender awareness initiated by the UN organisations and national governments in the global conferences on gender issues held in Mexico in 1975, Nairobi in 1985 and Beijing in 1995. These developments have been well-documented (Pietila and Vickers, 1995; Jain, 2006). The continuous research, debate and advocacy resulting from these collaborations and encounters have led to a significant focus on gender mainstreaming in development.

Defining Gender Mainstreaming

Gender mainstreaming broadly refers to the transformation of structures of power within institutions that determine the allocation of public resources through policy formulation and implementation. Put simply, bringing gender into the mainstream means making gender equality goals 'key decision-making criteria that are pursued from the centre, rather than the margins' (Odora-Hoppers, 2005: 67). It has been argued by experts and academics over the past four decades that the benefits of development by-pass women when they are viewed as dependents within households, responsible for the maintenance of the home, but little else. Policy approaches that focus solely on women as mothers or carers of children confirmed the unequal treatment of women within families and communities, where they were treated as unpaid workers within the family.

The Women in Development (WID) movement emerged from a well-developed critique of the more narrowly conceived approach to addressing women's interests, particularly in aid programmes, but also in national policy and programming in many countries. Noting that a 'welfare' approach was predominantly used to target women, WID fought for a shift in thinking in development policy towards approaches that recognise and value the productive contributions of women, both paid and unpaid, as well as the enormous amount of work they do in the domestic sphere, reproducing families in the vital areas of food provision, childcare and child rearing. The under-valuation of this labour, as argued in Chapter 2, has led to systematic under-investment in women's capacities and well-being by households, communities and states.

WID approaches have themselves evolved over the years through iterative processes of debate, research and practice, and have given way to the now commonly used terminology of gender and development (GAD). GAD signifies a move away from emphasising 'women' as a discrete developmental target group towards understanding that the very categories of 'woman' and 'man' emerge from a set of underlying social processes and structures that, through the creation of these identities, reinforces socially constructed differences that are then reproduced over and over again in the dynamics of every-day life. An emphasis on women alone is insufficient for an understanding of the dynamics of power and the reproduction of inequality; GAD points to the importance of focusing on the dynamics and processes inherent in the relationship *between* women *and* men in society.

Thus a GAD approach emphasises the importance of under-standing the underlying social 'rules' (Kabeer, 1999b) which lead both women and men to accept and reinforce an unequal social order resulting in, for example, the under-investment in the education of daughters or, more broadly, son-preference. By emphasising processes and social dynamics, GAD's approach implies the need to move beyond merely targeting women as a response, and instead requires a focus on the transformation of underlying social dynamics and processes through challenging social 'rules' that uphold inequality and injustice.

Gender mainstreaming, as it has evolved through changes in thinking and shifts from WID to GAD, thus has two broad strategies, to be followed simultaneously. The first is a focus on the transformation of the underlying rules and norms that rein-force inequality through 'naturalising' what are actually socially constructed differences. The second is a recognition that in order to start redressing inequalities, a targeted focus on women will be necessary to correct historical imbalances in investment in women's capacities and well-being. These are not mutually exclusive approaches, but are both necessary to effect transformation. Empowering women requires pro-

An emphasis on women alone is insufficient for an understanding of the dynamics of power and the reproduction of inequality ...

Empowering women requires programmes and resources directed at ... providing spaces for them to practice leadership and make their voices heard, so that they can drive change according to their own visions of what is desirable and possible.

grammes and resources directed at developing women's inherent capacities and providing spaces for them to practice leadership and make their voices heard, so that they can drive change according to their own visions of what is desirable and possible. Equally, micro-level processes of change need to be supported by changes in the wider policy environment and in the institutions that structure and resource opportunities for women and men in order to create substantive equality.

In emphasising the importance of public policy in enabling and sustaining change for equality, gender mainstreaming has necessarily focused on transforming the state and its institutions of law, policy and administration. Public policy can be instrumental in sending out messages about the kind of society and the kinds of outcomes that are desired by members of a nation state. When laws and policies are discriminatory, they reinforce social biases and reduce spaces for individuals to challenge inequalities operating in their lives. Where laws and policies are progressive and based on conceptions of well-being that, in turn, embody ideas of equality and rights, they provide spaces for individuals to challenge inequities and claim rights.

As Box 6.1 shows, the transformation of development policies within the apparatus of the state has been attempted in many countries through the development of special machinery, such as separate departments or ministries within government, charged with the task of ensuring that a gender perspective is brought into all public policy actions of government and that special programmes and investments target women in particular. The strategies are complementary rather than mutually exclusive. Projects and programmes for women must be sited within a wider transformative approach to policies and implementation structures in order to move forward the agenda for gender equality and justice.

As Razavi and Miller (1995) note, this twofold approach to transformation is extremely challenging and demanding. Given the difficulties of entering and changing entrenched institutions such as bureaucracies, which by their nature are opaque and intensely rule-bound, *'the task of transformation is often, by necessity, downplayed or postponed'* (Byrne *et al.*, 1996). Advocacy for gender mainstreaming becomes difficult: if it is promoted as a political issue it can provoke hostility among the very people who are being sought as agents of change within bureaucratic systems. If, on the other hand, it is promoted as a technical issue which can be 'fixed' with a few simple tools, it can reduce a progressive agenda for change into a banal exercise with little meaning. Striking the balance between the analytical and technical skills required for change, as well as winning allies for what can often be perceived as a long-drawn out social struggle, remains a challenge.

Given the state's central mandate in relation to gender mainstreaming, attention has been focused both on state actions vis-à-vis gender inequalities in society as well as state actions vis-à-vis gender inequalities within its own structures and operation. Where the state itself reflects wider gender inequalities through its recruitment policies, postings and treatment of women staff, its actions vis-à-vis wider society are also likely to be flawed. For example, a survey carried out among members of the Indian Administrative Service in 1995 reveals a range of findings about the nature of the gendered structures of state institutions (Thakur, 1999). Women are often denied important posts, or have to fight for them, and are more likely to get what are considered 'soft' postings in departments and ministries which have relatively little symbolic power and authority. Gender mainstreaming has thus required an internal focus for the state in relation to its own institutions of the executive, legislature and judiciary.

Where the state itself reflects wider gender inequalities through its recruitment policies, postings and treatment of women staff, its actions vis-à-vis wider society are also likely to be flawed.

Strategies for Mainstreaming Gender Equality

Influencing state institutions has largely been seen as a matter of getting bureaucratic institutions to take on a commitment to gender equality. The placement of units and focal points for 'gender' within ministries has been a leading strategy to institutionalise gender concerns in the policies and actions of a range of sectoral departments. However, as has been well documented (Goetz, 1997), these women's 'machineries' have often been weak, under-resourced, and vulnerable to changing political fortunes and co-option by political parties (Moser, 1993). Moreover, the agenda to effect change through 'technical' means seems to have yielded few results in the absence of measures for changing the mindsets of overwhelmingly male-dominated organisations which have little incentive to do things differently.

Box 6.2 Common Problems in Gender Mainstreaming through National Machineries

- Lack of a strong mandate to enforce compliance

- Lack of autonomy to drive change

- Poor capacity of selected focal points

- Locational instability caused by frequent changes in the way mainstreaming is attempted

- Underfunding, resulting in allocations that are disproportionate for the scale of the task

- Resistance from peers and counterparts, resulting in lack of compliance

- Underdeveloped monitoring and tracking tools, leading to insufficient knowledge about the impact of programmes aimed at achieving gender equality

Byrne *et al.,* 1996

Technical inputs included checklists and guidelines, and gender awareness training to help orient staff to the new requirements of a 'gender-sensitive approach'. While these tools did much to make administrators and policy-makers gender aware, they did little to locate the need for change within wider societal processes of inequality and their consequences for women and implications for men, and did not encourage trainees to recognise the wider mandate of equality embedded in most constitutions, and what this meant for the jobs they were doing.

Approaches to gender-awareness training have undergone many changes, as feminist advocates recognised that the approach to training required an orientation towards the society within which administrators functioned. There is also a need to bring the categories of 'man' and 'woman' to life within particular social and personal contexts. To make a real change, a thoughtful approach to complex societal relations and processes is required. However, advocates of gender equality are still often asked to reduce these complicated social realities to the lowest common explanatory denominators, resulting in tools and guidelines that often dilute the urgency or intensity with which change needs to be sustained.

A recent report by the UK Department for International Development (DFID), synthesising findings from an evaluation of its gender mainstreaming strategy, suggests that part of the problem is that development practitioners perceive that the commitment to gender equality is in 'competition with other development objectives' (DFID, 2006: xi). Arguing the case for an approach to development that both recognises the importance of social equality and at the same time emphasises rapid growth, investment, scaling up of services and opportunities is a challenging task, as the trade-offs required to achieve the latter are often at the expense of the former.

A second problem, associated with many agencies, is also noted in the DFID report: procedures and guidelines developed to ensure gender mainstreaming are often considered optional rather than mandatory, and are therefore unevenly implemented. Where measures to secure and check compliance are not strongly developed, gender mainstreaming strategies are likely to remain on paper rather than being put into practice.

The particular dilemma that emerges with relation to gender mainstreaming is how to balance the need for pragmatism to ensure that all policies and programmes take gender inequalities into account and address them, with the need for a paradigm change in the way that development planning and policy formulation is undertaken. For policies to yield 'parity effects' in education, there needs to be sectoral effectiveness in planning the distribution of infrastructure and human resources to improve supply, and well-targeted incentives and broad-based community involvement to ensure demand-side participation. These are amenable to mainstreaming gender targets across all aspects of planning, as they can be based on numerical measurements (for example the number of girls out of school or the numbers of villages with inadequate school infrastructure).

However, in order to generate 'equality effects', policies need to engage more with the issues of gender identity and social relations that lead to biased curriculum development and curricular transaction, and to peer relations that reinforce boys' perception of greater privilege relative to girls. It also requires attention to linkages beyond the sector – recognising

The particular dilemma ... is how to balance the need for pragmatism to ensure that all policies and programmes take gender inequalities into account ... with the need for a paradigm change in the way that development planning and policy formulation is undertaken.

Box 6.3 **Gender Mainstreaming Strategies within DFID**

The UK Government's Department for International Development has been a leader in shaping the discourse on gender equality and women's empowerment, and has recently looked within the organisation for evidence of the existence and effectiveness of its own internal gender mainstreaming strategies. A desk review by Watkins (2004) shows a range of different strategies in place in different countries and within headquarters:

- Gender reviews of the portfolio of programmes;

- Markers and mechanisms to track gender commitments within programmes;

- Gender training;

- Information and resource support units to feed information as required to support programming;

- Gender audits to check internal work;

- Gender strategies for country programme development;

- Support for gender budgets and poverty reduction strategy processes.

Specialist advisers in the form of social development advisers provide a cadre of professionals tasked with examining the gender and other social dimensions of all programming.

However, the desk review of the impact of these strategies shows that they have been used to varying degrees in different country programmes, and that they have often been implemented unevenly. More importantly, the review points to the poor documentation of effective main-streaming practices and the resulting difficulty of evaluating their impact. However, the final evaluation report (DFID, 2006) finds that of all the sectors of DFID work, gender is most consistently reflected in education sector programmes.

Watkins, 2004; DFID, 2006

that education both influences and is influenced by developments in the wider environment, be it in the area of family structure and investment in girls' development or with respect to the labour market and its encouragement of women's participation, thereby generating demand for education at post-primary and secondary levels. These require policy environments that are creative, forward-looking, socially conscious and open to new ideas.

The need for new political will to make the wider vision of gender equality become a reality is urgent if gender mainstreaming strategies are to be effective. Subrahmanian (2005b) identifies three interlinked limitations associated with gender mainstreaming strategies so far: analytical, institutional and political. Poor thinking translates into poor action and in turn reinforces low political will to make a change. If any of these components are missing, there is likely to be only a limited push for meaningful change.

The role of politics is critical in a context where much is known about what needs to be done to achieve goals (World Bank, 2004). Girls' education has received considerable attention in the last few years, and a significant amount of knowledge has been gathered about 'what works' in promoting it. Attention now needs to be paid to systemic reform issues and the politics and costs associated with achieving this reform. However, as Rose and Subrahmanian (2005) note, as much of the pressure for gender parity and equality in education is driven by external processes, for example the MDGs, EFA, poverty reduction strategy papers (PRSPs), sector wide approaches (SWAps) and fast track initiatives (FTIs), governments prefer investing in showcase projects that can visibly demonstrate that they are acting on these issues, rather than doing the long, slow and often invisible work of mainstreaming gender across sectors, plans and policies. This results in disjunctures between philosophy (a commitment to mainstreaming) and practice (simple visible projects where the headcount of women is high).

Short-term gains – and gender parity gains in relation to universal primary education (UPE) are easily won given the high demand for female primary schooling – are always likely to score higher on the policy agenda than long-term gains built on the foundations of complex change, especially in demo-

The need for new political will to make the wider visions of gender equality become a reality is urgent if gender mainstreaming strategies are to be effective.

Short-term gains ... are always likely to score higher on the policy agenda than long-term gains built on the foundations of complex change.

cratic societies. Countries may prefer to keep innovative projects parallel to the main programme so that these remain attractive to funders and they can raise funds specifically for them. An evaluation study of the Africa Girls' Education Initiative (Chapman *et al.*, 2003) revealed that there was concern that if strategies for girls' education were fully mainstreamed they might be invisible and so not fundable by donors. This raises issues also about donor criteria and the incentives that may be needed to ensure mainstreaming of innovations for girls' education as part of the education system as a whole.

Critical capacities that can bridge the gap between the conceptual advances made by gender advocates and the institutional mindsets that characterise policy-making bureaucracies are still lacking in many countries and organisations. While there are high-powered gender bodies within the World Bank, for example, capacity is unevenly distributed. There is an increasingly high level of awareness of the importance of gender but, as in other agencies, there are institutional difficulties in translating this into a coherent strategy. Odora-Hoppers (2005: 60) argues that women and gender specialists often lack the tactical skills required to negotiate the policy-making arena and its complex dimensions, and that appointments to head specialist gender units or sections *'rarely follow technically rigid criteria that can guarantee strong and concise delivery'*. Gender specialists are likely to face a double bind: they are required to transform entire bureaucracies single-handedly, while at the same time occupying positions considered so specialist that they have no clearly defined career path. Developing critical policy skills and capacities alongside defining clear career paths with incentives to both promote gender specialists into non-specialists and also encourage non-specialists to acquire gender skills need to go hand-in-hand. This is necessary to avoid the trap that Diop (2004: 9) identifies in Rwanda, where she notes that both line ministries and public institutions continue to consider that *'the operationalisation of the promotion of gender equality is the sole duty of the Ministry of Gender and Family Promotion'*, despite efforts to mainstream gender across different ministries.

Box 6.4 **Strategies to Strengthen Gender Mainstreaming within Government**

- Autonomous oversight bodies with legislated mandates and independent members – in countries where there is free press, even if they are not taken seriously by policy-makers, they can use the media to highlight issues and concerns and thereby put pressure on governments.

- External bodies constituted by local organisations supported by international movements and deliberative processes.

- Senior bureaucrats as gender focal points – in practice, focal points have been junior staff who receive limited attention from within the system and have no authority to make recommendations or even speak at meetings. If seniority becomes the selection principle, it will reverse perceptions of the importance of such posts, and publicised failures to pursue the mandate provided can cause greater embarrassment and thus create an incentive to work for change, if motivation is weak.

- Clearly mapped career paths and other incentives for those who work as gender focal points.

- Focal points located at all levels of the delivery structure, not just in a planning function. A chain of command all the way to the field with a clear oversight and monitoring function would enable field level realities to be highlighted to senior managers and policy-makers on a regular basis, and provide a forum for finding solutions and answers to constraints that are locally specific.

Bringing large numbers of women into political and policy systems is critical for creating the 'mass' required to make a difference. However, these changes alone are not sufficient. For many governments, visible programmes of affirmative action become both the starting point (which they are), as well as the end point (which they should not be) of policy initiatives aimed at gender equality.

In the final analysis, change towards gender equality is likely to be the product of many dimensions of social action, whether deliberate or unintentional. The role of public policy is to give shape to such change, and to hasten it through creating appropriate frameworks in the form of norms, standards and opportunities. The international development community has now accepted that narrowly focused change processes – whether in particular sectors or access measures – need to give way to broader approaches in the areas of gender equality in order to sustain gains generated from short-term measures. This means widening the sphere of activity for gender mainstreaming advocacy to include areas such as building infrastructure, and economic and trade policy, as well as expanding the range of interventions used to further this important goal.

Box 6.5 Gender-responsive Budget Analysis

One of the most powerful tools to emerge from gender mainstreaming strategies is 'gender budgeting' – allowing feminist advocates to engage with planners and economists on their own terrain, using their language and analyses to open up spaces for discussing the interests of women in relation to policy-making and planning.

Gender budgets in particular have been strongly promoted as an opportunity to move out of the very limiting notions of women and development that were restricted to traditional line departments concerned with women or family affairs. Advocates of gender equality called for 'a broadening of the role of government budgeting in all sectors, and advocate using government budgeting to reduce inequality in both economic and social contexts' (Sarraf, 2003). This new approach involves not only central government agencies, but also sectoral ministries and local government.

Unlike aid modalities, gender budgeting is a tool that was first developed by national governments and is now part of the toolkit that international agencies are promoting to

---

further gender analysis in planning processes. Pioneered in Australia, and now widely used in developed countries and more recently in developing countries, Gender Responsive Budget Analysis takes a systematic approach to planning, starting with policy appraisal and then moving to disaggregating public expenditure analysis, followed by beneficiary assessments in terms of the reach of public expenditure. The focus on budget analysis is comple-mented by attention to both backward and forward linkages with a view to understanding the policy design elements that give rise to particular allocation patterns and then assessing the impact of expenditures on outcomes for women and men.

Coherent and systematic gender analysis of each of these aspects should result in more effective gender-aware development planning. In addition, gender budgets have been promoted as a tool that can help governments and international agencies map the extent to which gender commitments are translated into specific and traceable outcomes, so that budgets can be adjusted to reflect these commitments and their implementation (Sarraf, 2003).

These support overall efforts to promote budgetary reform through the articulation of Medium Term Expenditure Frameworks, which seek to plan expenditure on the basis of assessment of current and future revenue and expenditure streams.

However, as with all mainstreaming initiatives, much depends on how gender budgeting tools are embedded within the overall planning process. Diop (2004) points out that gender budget exercises are still largely perceived as requiring a disaggregation of allocations earmarked for women, rather than reflecting an understanding of the importance of developing methods for analysing and interpreting the gender-disaggregated impacts of resource allocations.

Mainstreaming Gender in the New International Aid Architecture

New mechanisms for aid delivery have emerged out of a concern with the limited effectiveness of project approaches and the belief in the greater efficiency of resource pooling between donors and strengthened processes of debate and dialogue about key areas of priorities with governments. Bringing the state back into the picture has meant that issues of national ownership have been framed as central objectives of these new policy tools.

Poverty reduction strategies (PRS) are the cornerstone of new aid modalities for debt relief in heavily indebted poor countries (HIPCs), though they are now being used in non-HIPC countries as well. PRS have been touted as a success of gender advocacy, in that gender issues are highlighted as central to national poverty reduction strategies and the poverty reduction strategy papers (PRSPs) developed by countries eligible for funding under this initiative are required to include detailed gender analysis in their analysis of poverty, and in their planning and expenditure for development. Rodenberg (2002: 2) notes that the approach to gender in the PRS process draws on a wider 'win-win' scenario articulated in international development discourse, that sees *'a high level of reciprocity between greater gender equity, economic growth, and effective poverty reduction'*.

Four elements are central to the development of a PRSP (Rodenberg, 2002):

- Comprehensive poverty analysis;

- Clearly specified priorities for planned structural economic reforms and social programmes;

- Adequate targets and indicators for the process of implementation and monitoring;

- Description of the participatory process that led to the preparation of a PRSP.

From a gender perspective, each of these elements represents a crucial aspect of the gender mainstreaming agenda, and in particular offers an opportunity for ensuring that greater resources are better targeted at the interests and needs of women. Education, in the PRS process, has been emphasised as a key social sector that needs to complement macroeconomic growth strategies and structural reforms.

In their review of six World Bank Poverty Assessments from four sub-Saharan African countries (Ghana, Zambia, Tanzania and Uganda), Whitehead and Lockwood (1999) note a range of limitations in gender analysis, including variations in the way in which the language of 'gender and development' is used and the different methodologies used to measure and define poverty (see also Bamberger *et al.*, 2002). Their analysis and findings are not dissimilar to the findings of the review of PRSPs cited above. However, and importantly, they link the poverty of the gender analysis to overall weaknesses in the commitment and capacities of the World Bank with respect to gender issues. By perpetuating the long institutionalised association of women with 'human resources', the Bank's central mandate and concern with economic growth issues have remained parity focused. The diversity of methodologies and approaches used can be partly explained by the weak operational guidelines prepared by the Bank in helping national teams develop their assessments (Whitehead and Lockwood, 1999).

Sector wide approaches to development cooperation involve donor support to the development of an entire sector in a given country (OECD-DAC, 2002). As distinct from a project-based approach, donors pool resources to support an entire sector, backing financial support with technical and planning support. An intrinsic part of coordinated support is the use of common procedures. SWAps are different from budgetary support, discussed earlier, in that a SWAp *'typically contains a mix of project aid and other modalities, the bulk of which is not disbursed through government systems'* (Hoole, 2002: 1).

Building partnerships between donors and other stakeholders, including governments, SWAps have the following components:

- An overall sector policy framework;

- Priorities and objectives (strategy) and performance measures;

- Expenditure programmes;

... there are significant barriers to the promotion of equal rights for women and men within policy-making institutions ...

- Institutional reform and capacity building needed for implementation;

- Jointly agreed management, reporting and accounting arrangements.

Some of the gender issues raised in relation to SWAps are similar to those raised for PRSPs. An OECD-DAC review (2002: 4) notes that in most cases they focus on *'narrowly defined investments in women or girls rather than addressing the underlying conditions that produce unequal access for males and females'*. Further, without active and effective 'champions', gender equality issues tend to disappear off the agenda. The dilemma of specialist gender personnel was also raised – having specific posts for gender specialists tends to leave them isolated and removes the onus of gender-awareness work from other staff; but not having specialist staff means that gender disappears as a visible agenda issue. The OECD-DAC Working Party on Gender Equality, in its review of donor support for gender equality in education (1999), noted that there was much confusion regarding the concept of mainstreaming among agency staff working in the education field.

In a major study carried out for DFID, Sibbons *et al.* (2000) observe that access issues are emphasised over quality concerns and that the strategies being promoted have implications for promoting girls' education. For example, they note that by emphasising primary education, rather than post-basic education, the threshold appears to be set very low, which demotivates parents from educating girls.

The review of gender mainstreaming in PRSPs and SWAps thus highlights that much remains the same with respect to gender despite new avenues for policy influence and easier entry points, particularly in relation to education. There is no resistance to 'gender parity talk' and gender equality has become part of the lexicon of education policy, albeit to a far smaller extent. As pointed out above, nowhere in the Dakar documents has gender equality been defined. This suggests that there are significant barriers to the promotion of equal rights for women and men within policy-making institutions; these need to be the subject of deeper analysis.

The Fast Track Initiative (FTI) mandated by the Monterrey

Consensus of 2002 aims at promoting new development partnerships with the MDGs as a frame of reference. Within this compact, countries that implement policy and institutional reforms and prove their performance record are rewarded with additional aid and better coordinated external assistance for their education plans. It is clear that the attainment of the EFA goals requires a substantial increase in aid to basic education. However, aid alone will be insufficient. Increased financial transfers to countries which have poor policies and a weak institutional environment are unlikely to pay dividends for EFA. History also shows that the diffuse objectives of agencies, the different modalities under which aid is provided and its poor coordination within developing countries often undermine aid effectiveness. The recent inception and development of the FTI, designed to help achieve universal primary education by 2015, has highlighted the difficulties of achieving a more effective use of international resources, whether they take the form of financial flows or technical assistance.

The FTI is a response to the sense of urgency created by the World Education Forum. Underpinning it is a simulation model that provides the framework for evaluation of the proposals submitted, which in turn is based on the experience of countries that have successfully achieved or made progress towards UPE. As many of the countries which came forward for inclusion had only a small proportion of the world's out-of-school children, an analytical fast track has been developed to build capacity for acceleration in five high population countries. The Analytical FTI (AFT) was particularly promoted by DFID because of its concern that by focusing on rewarding only those countries that had 'credible' plans, the FTI was in danger of only funding countries that were already receiving aid and were established 'good performers' (DFID, 2002, cited in Rose, 2003).

Like the PRSPs and the SWAp frameworks, the FTI framework has been criticised for failing to go beyond a limited parity focus in setting the benchmarks for funding (Rose, 2005). However, Unterhalter (2007) notes that a recent UN Girls' Education Initiative (UNGEI) review of the FTI in 2005 has taken up the issue of its weak regulatory framework in promoting gender issues in the achievement of education goals. In particular, the lack of oversight exerted over country plans that

The recent inception and development of the FTI ... has highlighted the difficulties of achieving a more effective use of international resources, whether they take the form of financial flows or technical assistance.

... policy-making processes have to be made transparent and inclusive at all levels to ensure both that resources are allocated to meet priority gaps and needs, and that diverse voices are heard ...

have paid little attention to gender and yet have received endorsement has been flagged as an issue of concern. Acting on this report, the need for a comprehensive approach to gender equality has been agreed, which Unterhalter regards as a positive response to a critique from the UN initiative mandated to scrutinise all aspects of gender mainstreaming among donor and government partners.

Assessments of gender budgets, SWAps and PRSPs point to similar and continuing problems with respect to the mainstreaming of gender issues. While these modalities create explicit mandates for dealing with gender, there are continuing limitations of analysis and understanding of what gender mainstreaming entails. Rose and Subrahmanian (2005) note that even PRSPs that make a reference to gender inequality (for example that of Malawi) are often light on analysis of the issues that underlie it and tend to suggest isolated or targeted actions which are quantifiable.

Gender may have become more visible in all of these new aid modalities, but the capacity and political space within which this visibility can be translated into coherent and consistent analyses and action are still lacking. Reviews of PRS processes, as well as of other international aid instruments, modalities and normative statements, show that in all of them the understanding of gender continues to be expressed in terms of separate allocations for women within overall development processes.

Conclusion

While successful and comprehensive mainstreaming strategies continue to elude seekers of progress on commitments to gender equality, there is a need to move beyond expecting national and international bureaucracies to lead on this front. Clearly, more complex societal understandings of gender inequality are not easily amenable to bureaucratic modes of planning and implementation that require numerical quantification and clearly deliverable targets. Without partnerships with actors who represent diverse societal processes located across the geographical spectrum, these disjunctures are likely to remain. A significant conclusion must therefore be that policy-making processes have to be made transparent and inclusive at all levels to ensure both that resources are allocated to meet priority gaps and needs, and that diverse voices are heard in promoting social equality. Policy-making institutions need to institutionalise such partnerships, which can also contribute to holding public institutions accountable. Where public policies can play a role is in developing strong frameworks of commitment to gender equality and in monitoring progress towards these in a systematic and rigorous way.

References

Alsop, R. and Heinsohn, N. (2005). 'Measuring Empowerment in Practice: Structuring Analysis and Framing Indicators', World Bank Policy Research Working Paper 3510. Washington, DC: World Bank.

American Association of University Women (1992). 'How Schools Shortchange Girls: A Study of Major Findings on Girls and Education'. Washington, DC: AAUW.

Ansell, Nicola (2002). 'Secondary Education Reform in Lesotho and Zimbabwe and the Needs of Rural Girls: pronouncements, policy and practice', *Comparative Education* 38(1): 91–112.

Arnot, M. and Phipps, A. (2003). 'Gender and Education in the UK', Background Paper for *EFA Global Monitoring Report, 2003/4*. Paris: UNESCO.

Avalos, B. (2003). 'Gender Parity and Equality in Chile: A Case Study', Background Paper for *EFA Global Monitoring Report, 2003/4*. Paris: UNESCO.

Baden, S. and Greene, C. (1994). 'Gender and Education in Asia and the Pacific', BRIDGE Report No. 25. Brighton, UK: Institute of Development Studies.

Bailey, B. (2003). 'Gender-sensitive educational policy and practice: the case of Jamaica', Background Paper for *EFA Global Monitoring Report 2003/04*. Paris: UNESCO.

Bamberger, M., Blackden, M., Fort, L. and Manoukian, V. (2002). 'Gender' in Klugman, J. (ed.), *A Sourcebook for Poverty Reduction Strategies*. Washington, DC: World Bank.

Barrientos, Armando and DeJong, Jocelyn (2004). 'Child Poverty and Cash Transfers', CHIP Report No. 4, Childhood Poverty Research and Policy Centre. London: Save the Children.

Baudino, C. (2003). 'Case Study: France', Background Paper for *EFA Global Monitoring Report 2003/04*. Paris: UNESCO.

Bennell, P. (2003). 'Public-Private Partnerships in Basic Education in South Asia', Paper prepared for Seminar on Public-Private Partnerships for the Delivery of Basic Education Services to the Poor, London, 25 September 2003. London: Aga Khan Foundation and Department for International Development, UK.

Benson, C. (2005). *Girls, Educational Equity and Mother Tongue-based Teaching*. Bangkok: UNESCO.

Bhalotra, S. (2000). 'Is child work necessary?', Econometric Society World Congress 2000, Manchester, Working Papers in Economics No. 0500.

Blackmore, J. (2004). 'Gender equity and resourcing reflections Australia', Paper presented at the Beyond Access Forum, Oxford, 28 April 2004.

Blaug, M. (1987). *The Economics of Education and the Education of an Economist*. London: Edward Elgar Publishing.

Bray, M. (1998). 'Financing Education in Developing Asia: Themes, Tensions, and Policies', *International Journal of Educational Research* 29(7): 627–42.

Britto, T. (2005). *Recent trends in the development agenda of Latin America: an analysis of conditional cash transfers*. Manchester: Institute for Development Policy and Management.

Byrne, B., Koch-Leier, J., Baden, S. and Marcus, R. (1996). 'National machineries for women in development: experiences, lessons and strategies for institutionalising gender in development policy and planning', Report No. 36, BRIDGE. Brighton: Institute of Development Studies, University of Sussex.

Chapman, D.W., Kyeyune, R. and Lokkesmoe, K. (2003). 'Evaluation of the African Girls Education Initiative. Country Case Study: Uganda', mimeo. New York: UNICEF.

Colclough, C., Al-Samarrai, S., Rose, P. and Tembon, M. (2003). *Achieving Schooling for All in Africa: Costs, Commitment and Gender*. Aldershot, UK: Ashgate.

—— (1997). 'Education, health and the market: An introduction', in Colclough, C. (ed.), *Marketizing Education and Health in Developing Countries: Miracle or Mirage?*. Oxford: Clarendon Press.

Collard, D. (1999). 'The Generational Bargain', Paper presented at conference of the Development Studies Association, 'The Inter-Generational Bargain', University of Bath, 12–14 September.

Commonwealth Secretariat (2005). *Promising Practices and Implications for Scaling Up Girls' Education*, Report of the UN Girls' Education Initiative South Asia Workshop, held in Chandigarh, India, 20–22 September 2004. London: Commonwealth Secretariat and New Delhi: UNICEF.

De Janvry, A., Finan, F., Sadoulet, E. and Vakis, R. (2004). 'Can conditional cash transfers serve as safety nets to keep children at school and out of the labor market?'. Berkeley: University of California.

DFID (2006). *Evaluation of DFID's Policy and Practice in Support of Gender Equality and Women's Empowerment*, Vol. I, Synthesis Report, Evaluation Report EV669. London: DFID.

Diop, Ngone (2004). 'Gender Budgeting in Education Ministries. The Case study of the Rwanda Ministry of Education', Paper presented at the Beyond Access workshop, 28–29 April 2004. London: Institute of Education; Oxford: Oxfam UK.

Drèze, Jean and Sen, Amartya (2002). *India: Development and Participation*. Oxford: Oxford University Press.)

—— (1995). *India: Economic Development and Selected Regional Perspectives*. New Delhi: Oxford University Press.

Dunne, M. and Leach, F. (2005). 'Gendered School Experiences: the impact on retention and achievement in Botswana and Ghana', Researching the Issues 56. London: Department for International Development.

ECLAC and UNIFEM (1995). *Regional Programme of Action for the Women of Latin America and the Caribbean 1995–2001*. Santiago, Chile.

Eloundou-Enyegue, P.M. (2004). 'Pregnancy-Related Dropouts and Gender Inequality in Education: A Life-Table Approach and Application to Cameroon', *Demography* 41(3): 509–28.

Fentiman, A., Hall, A. and Bundy, D. (1999). 'School Enrolment Patterns in Rural Ghana: a comparative study of the impact of location, gender, age and health on children's access to basic schooling', *Comparative Education* 35(3): 331–49.

Figueroa, M. (2000). 'Making sense of male experience: the case of academic underachievement in the English-speaking Caribbean', *IDS Bulletin* 31(2): 68–74. Brighton: Institute of Development Studies, University of Sussex.

Folbre, N. (1994). *Who Pays for the Kids?: Gender and the Structures of Constraint*. London: Routledge.

Fransman, J., Irvine, R. and Wahby, Y. (2003). 'Can gender parity lead to gender equity – Bangladesh country profile', Background paper for EFA Global Monitoring Report 2003/4. Paris: UNESCO.

Fuller, B. and Liang, X. (1999). 'Which Girls Stay in School? The Influence of Family Economy, Social Demands, and Ethnicity in South Africa', in Bledsoe, C.H., Casterline, J.B., Johnson-Kuhn, J.A. and Haaga, J.G. (eds), *Critical Perspectives on Schooling and Fertility in the Developing World*. Washington, DC: National Academy Press.

Gardener, J. and Subrahmanian, R. (2005). 'Tackling Social Exclusion in Health and Education in South Asia', Report for DFID Asia Division. London: GHK International and Brighton: Institute of Development Studies, University of Sussex.

Goetz, Anne-Marie (ed.) (1997). *Getting institutions right for women in development*. London: Zed Books.

Hargreaves, J. and Boler, T. (2006). *Girl power: the impact of girls' education on HIV and sexual behaviour*. London: ActionAid International.

Hashim, Iman (2005). 'Exploring the Linkages between Children's Independent Migration and Education: Evidence from Ghana', Working Paper T12, Sussex Centre for Migration Research. Brighton: University of Sussex.

Herz, B. and Sperling, G. (2004). *What Works in Girls' Education. Evidence and Policies from the Developing World.* New York: Council on Foreign Relations.

Heward, C. (1999). 'Introduction: The New Discourses of Gender, Education and Development' in Heward, C. and Bunwaree, S. (eds.), *Gender, Education and Development: Beyond Access to Empowerment.* London: Zed Books.

Hoole, D. (2002). 'General Budget Support: Characteristics, Rationale and Experiences', Note for European Forum on Rural Development Cooperation, Montpellier, 4–6 September.

Human Rights Watch (2001). *Scared at School: Sexual Violence Against Girls in South African Schools.* New York, Washington, London and Brussels: Human Rights Watch.

Jain, D. (2006). *Women, Development, and the UN. A Sixty-Year Quest for Equality and Justice*, United Nations Intellectual History Project Series. Bloomington and Indianapolis: Indiana University Press.

Jain, S. (2004). 'Adhyapika Manch: A Case Study', Paper presented at the Workshop on Promising Practices and Implications for Scaling up Girls' Education, Chandigarh, India, 20–23 September 2004. London: Commonwealth Secretariat.

—— (2003). 'Gender equality in education: community-based initiatives in India' Background paper for EFA Global Monitoring Report 2003–04. Paris: UNESCO.

Jeffery, R. and Basu, A.M. (1996). 'Schooling as Contraception?' in Jeffery, R. and Basu, A.M. (eds), *Girls' Schooling, Women's Autonomy and Fertility Change in South Asia.* New Delhi: Sage Publications.

Jeffery, R. and Jeffery, P. (1998). 'Silver bullet or passing fancy? Girls' schooling and population policy', in Jackson, C. and Pearson, R. (eds), *Feminist Visions of Development: Gender Analysis and Policy.* London/New York: Routledge.

Jejeebhoy, S. (1995). *Women's Education, Autonomy and Reproductive Behaviour: Experiences from Developing Countries.* Oxford: Clarendon Press.

Jha, J. and Subrahmanian, R. (2006). 'Secondary Education in the Indian State of Uttar Pradesh: Gender Dimensions of State Policy and Practice', in Razavi, S. and Hassim, S. (eds), *Gender and Social Policy in a Global Context: Mothers, Workers and Citizens.* Basingstoke: Palgrave.

Kaabwe, E.S.M. (2000). 'Establishing the pattern: gender and education in the African context', in Thody, A. and Kaabwe, E.S.M. (eds), *Educating Tomorrow: Lessons from Managing Girls' Education in Africa*. Kenwyn: Juta and Co. Ltd.

Kabeer, N. (2004). 'Re-visioning "the social": towards a citizen-centred social policy for the poor in poor countries', IDS Working Paper 191. Brighton: Institute of Development Studies, University of Sussex.

—— (2003). *Gender mainstreaming in poverty eradication and the millennium development goals: a handbook for policy-makers and other stakeholders*. London: Commonwealth Secretariat; Canada: International Development Research Centre.

—— (2001). *Discussing women's empowerment: theory and practice*. Stockholm: Swedish International Development Cooperation Agency.

—— (1999a). 'Resources, Agency, Achievement: Reflections on the Measurement of Women's Empowerment', *Development as Change* 30(3): 435–64.

—— (1999b). 'From concepts to practice: Gender-aware planning through the institutional framework', in Kabeer and Subrahmanian (eds), *Institutions, Relations and Outcomes. A Framework and Case Studies for Gender-aware Planning*. New Delhi: Kali for Women.

—— (1997). 'Tactics and trade offs: revisiting the links between gender and poverty', *IDS Bulletin* 28(3): 1–13. Brighton: Institute of Development Studies, University of Sussex.

—— (1994). *Reversed realities: gender hierarchies in development thought*. London: Verso.

—— and Subrahmanian, R. (eds) (1999). *Institutions, Relations and Outcomes. A Framework and Case Studies for Gender-aware Planning*. New Delhi: Kali for Women.

Kane, E. (2004). 'Girl's Education in Africa: What do we know about strategies that work?', Africa Region Human Development Working Paper Series no. 73. Washington, DC: World Bank.

King, E and Hill, A.M. (1993). 'Women's education in developing countries: An overview' in King, E. and Hill, A.M. (eds), *Women's Education in Developing Countries: Barriers, Benefits and Policies*. Baltimore and London: Johns Hopkins University Press for the World Bank.

Kingdon, G. (1998). 'Does the labour market explain lower female schooling in India?', *Journal of Development Studies* 35(1): 39, 65.

Kirk, J. (2003). 'Women in contexts of crisis: gender and conflict', Background paper for *EFA Global Monitoring Report 2003/4*. Paris: UNESCO.

Knodel, J. (1997). 'The closing of the gender gap in schooling: The case of Thailand', *Comparative Education* 33(1): 61, 86.

Lange, M.F. (2003). 'Gender inequality and education in Togo', Background paper for *EFA Global Monitoring Report 2003/4*. Paris: UNESCO.

Leach, F., Fiscian, V. and Kadzamira, E. (2003a). 'An investigative study of the abuse of girls in African schools', DFID Education research serials 54. London: DFID.

——, Dunne, M. and Humphreys, S. (2003b). 'Gender and Violence in Schools', Background paper for *EFA Global Monitoring Report 2003/4*. Paris: UNESCO.

Leclercq, F. (2003). 'Education Policy Reforms and the Quality of the School System: A Field Study of Primary Schools in Madhya Pradesh, India', DIAL, UR CIPRÉ – Université de Paris. Paris: Panthéon-Sorbonne.

Lee, W. (2002). 'Equity and Access to Education: Themes, Tensions and Policies', Asian Development Bank/Comparative Education Research Centre, University of Hong Kong.

Lewin, K. (1998). 'Education in Emerging Asia; Patterns Policies and Futures into the 21st Century' *International Journal of Educational Development* 18(2): 81–119.

Lloyd, C., Mete, C. and Sathar, Z. (2002). 'The Effect of Gender Differences in Primary School Access, Type, and Quality on the Decision to Enroll in Rural Pakistan', Working Paper No. 164, Policy Research Division. New York: Population Council.

Magno, C., Silova, I. and Wright, S. with Demeny, E. (2002). 'OPEN MINDS: Opportunities for gender equity in education in Central/South Eastern Europe and the former Soviet Union', mimeo. Budapest: Open Society Institute.

Male, J. (2000). 'Leaders and leadership for girls in coeducational schools: problems and prospects', in Thody, A. and Kaabwe, E.S.M. (eds), *Educating Tomorrow: Lessons from Managing Girls' Education in Africa*. Kenwyn: Juta and Co. Ltd.

Malhotra, A., Pande, R. and Grown, C. (2003). *Impact of Investments in Female Education on Gender Equality*. Washington, DC: International Center for Research on Women.

McNay, K. (2003). 'Women's changing roles in the context of the demographic transition', Background Paper for *EFA Global Monitoring Report 2003/4*. Paris: UNESCO.

Mehran, G. (2003). 'Gender and education in Iran', Background paper for *EFA Monitoring Report 2003/4*. Paris: UNESCO.

Miller, E. (2000). 'Education for All in the Caribbean in the 1990s: Retrospect and Prospect', in Quamina Aiyejina (ed.), *EFA in the Caribbean: Assessment 2000*, Monograph Series. Kingston, Jamaica: UNESCO.

Moore, K. (2001). 'Frameworks for understanding the intergenerational transmission of poverty and wellbeing in developing countries', CPRC Working Paper 8. Manchester: IDPM/Chronic Poverty Research Centre.

Morley, Samuel (2004). 'Cash for Education' in *Focus*, UNDP International Poverty Centre.

Moser, C. (1993). *Gender Planning and Development: Theory, Practice and Training*. London: Routledge.

Mturi, Akim J. (2003). 'Gender gap in school enrolment among youth in Lesotho', *Development Southern Africa*, 20 (4): 491–504.

Murthi, M. (2002). 'Fertility Change in Asia and Africa', *World Development* 30(10): 1769–78.

Nieuwenhuys, O. (1994). *Children's Lifeworlds: Gender, Welfare and Labour in the Developing World*. London and New York: Routledge.

Nussbaum, M. (2000). *Women and human development: the capabilities approach*. New Delhi: Kali for Women.

Odora-Hoppers, C. (2005). 'Between "mainstreaming" and "transformation": Lessons and challenges for institutional change', in Chisholm, L. and September, J. (eds), *Gender Equality in South African Education 1994–2004*, Conference proceedings. Cape Town: HSRC Press.

OECD-DAC (2002). *Gender Equality in Sector Wide Approaches: A Reference Guide*. Paris: Organisation for Economic Co-operation and Development, Development Assistance Committee.

—— (1999). 'Reaching the Goals in the S-21: Gender Equality and Education', Vol. I, Working Party on Gender Equality. Paris: Organisation for Economic Co-operation and Development, Development Assistance Committee.

Oxaal, Z. (1997). 'Education and Poverty: A Gender Analysis', Report No. 53. BRIDGE. (Brighton: Institute of Development Studies, University of Sussex.

Pietila, H. and Vickers, J. (1995). *Making Women Matter: The Role of the United Nations*. London: Zed Books.

Pilon, M. (2003). 'FosterCare and schooling in West Africa: the state of knowledge', Background Paper for *Global Monitoring Report 2003/4*. Paris: UNESCO.

Pratham (2005). *Annual Status of Education Report 2005*. New Delhi: Pratham.

PROBE (1999). *Public Report on Basic Education in India*. New Delhi: Oxford University Press.

Ramachandran, V. (2004). *Gender and Social Equity in Primary Education Hierarchies of Access*. New Delhi: Sage Publications.

—— (2003). 'Gender equality in education (India) – progress in the last decade', Background paper for *EFA Global Monitoring Report*. Paris: UNESCO.

Ramagoshi, M. (2005). 'National Department of Education Initiatives' in Chisholm, L. and September, J. (eds), *Gender Equity in South African Education 1994–2004*, Conference proceedings. Cape Town: HSRC Press.

Razavi, S. (2003). 'Women's changing roles in the context of economic reform and globalisation', Background paper for *EFA Monitoring Report 2003/4*. Paris: UNESCO.

—— and Miller, C. (1995). 'Gender Mainstreaming: A Study of Efforts by the UNDP, the World Bank and the ILO to Institutionalise Gender Issues', UNRSID Occasional Paper no. 4, Geneva.

Rodenberg, B. (2002). 'Integrating gender into poverty reduction strategies: from the declaration of intent to development policy in practice', Briefing Paper 2/2002. Bonn: German Development Institute.

Rose, P. (2005). 'Is there a "fast track" to achieving education for all?', *International Journal of Educational Development* 25(4): 381–94.

—— (2003). 'Tracking progress of the Fast Track Initiative: A Review of the FTI and indicative framework for education reform', Draft report for ActionAid on behalf of the Global Campaign for Education, mimeo. Sussex: Centre for International Education, University of Sussex.

Rose, P. and Al-Samarrai, S. (1997). 'Household Constraints on Schooling by Gender: Empirical Evidence from Ethiopia', Working Paper 56. Brighton: Institute of Development Studies, University of Sussex.

—— and Subrahmanian, R. (2005). 'Thematic Evaluation: Education', Evaluation of DFID Development Assistance: Gender Equality and Women's Empowerment, Phase II, Working Paper 11. London: DFID.

—— Tembon, M. (1997). 'Do Girls and Boys Benefit Equally as Enrolments Increase? Evidence from Two African Countries', Paper presented at the Conference on Education and Geopolitical Change, Oxford, 1997.

Saith, R. and Harriss-White, B. (1998). 'Gender Sensitivity of well-being Indicators', Discussion Paper No. 95. Geneva: UNRISD.

Sarraf, F. (2003). 'Gender-Responsive Government Budgeting', IMF Working Paper WP/03/83, Fiscal Affairs Department. Washington, DC: International Monetary Fund.

Sathar, Z. A., Lloyd, C. B., Mete, C. and ul Haque, M. (2003). 'Schooling opportunities for girls as a stimulus for fertility change in rural Pakistan', *Economic Development and Cultural Change* 51(3): 677–98.

Save the Children (2006). *Rewrite the Future: Education for children in conflict-affected countries*. London: International Save the Children Alliance.

—— (2003). 'Right of passage: harmful cultural practices and children's rights', Working Paper No. 25. London: International Save the Children Alliance.

Sen, Amartya K. (1995). 'Gender Inequality and Theories of Justice', in Nussbaum, M. and Glover, J. (eds), *Women, Culture and Development: A Study of Human Capabilities*. Oxford: Clarendon Press.

Sewell, T., Chavennes, B. and Morgan, S. (2003). 'Models for transformation of Jamaican schools: a study of masculinities, education and civil society', mimeo. University of Leeds, UK.

Sibbons, M., Smawfield, D., Poulsen, H., Gibbard, A., Norton, A. and Seel, A. (2000). 'Mainstreaing Gender through Sector Wide Approaches in education: synthesis report'. London: ODI; Cambridge: Cambridge Education Consultants.

Subrahmanian, R. (2005a). 'Gender Equality in Education: Definitions and Measurements', *International Journal of Educational Development* 25(4): 395–407.

—— (2005b). *'Scaling up' good practices in girls' education*. Paris: UNESCO.

—— (2002). *Gender and Education: A Review of Issues for Social Policy*. Geneva: United Nations Research in Social Development.

Tabor, Stephen (2002). 'Assisting the Poor with Cash: Design and Implementation of Social Transfer Programs', Social Protection Discussion Paper Series, No. 0223, (Social Protection Unit, Human Development Network. Washington DC: World Bank.

Tansel, A. (1997). 'Schooling attainment, parental education, and gender in Côte d'Ivoire and Ghana', *Economic Development and Cultural Change* 45(4): 825, 856.

Tembon, M. and Al-Samarrai, S. (1999). 'Who Gets Primary Schooling and Why? Evidence of Gender Inequalities Within Families in Guinea', Working Paper 85. Brighton: Institute of Development Studies, University of Sussex.

Thakur, S. (1999). '"More Equal than Others?" Gender Bias in the Constitution of Bureaucratic Merit in the Indian Administrative Service', in Kabeer, N. and Subrahmanian, R. (eds), *Institutions, Relations and Outcomes. A Framework and Case Studies for Gender-aware Planning*. New Delhi: Kali for Women.

Tietjen, K. (2003). 'The Bangladesh Primary Education Stipend Project: A Descriptive Analysis', mimeo. Washington, DC: World Bank.

Tilak, J.B.G. (1996). 'How Free is "Free" Primary Education in India?', *Economic and Political Weekly* 31 (5, 6): 275–82, 355–66.

Tomasevski, Katarina (2006). 'Free and compulsory education for all children: the gap between promise and performance', *Right to Education Primers, No. 2.*

UIS (2005). 'Children Out of School: Measuring Exclusion from Primary Education', Montreal: UNESCO Institute of Statistics.

UNESCO (2007). *Strong Foundations, Global Monitoring Report 2007.* Paris: UNESCO.

—— (2006). *Literacy for Life, Global Monitoring Report 2005/6.* Paris: UNESCO.

—— (2003). *Gender and Education for All: The Leap to Equality, Global Monitoring Report 2003/4.* Paris: UNESCO.

UNICEF (2003). *The State of the World's Children 2004: Girls, Education and Development.* New York: United Nations Children's Fund.

—— (1998). *The State of the World's Children 1999: Education.* New York: United Nations Children's Fund.

United Nations (1995). *Platform for Action of the Fourth World Conference on Women.* New York: United Nations.

UN Millenium Project (2005). 'Toward universal primary education: investments, incentives and institutions', Task Force on Education and Gender Equality. New York: UN Millennium Project.

Unterhalter, E. (2007). *Gender, Schooling and Global Social Justice.* London and New York: Routledge.

—— (2003). 'Education, capabilities and social justice', Paper prepared for *EFA Global Monitoring Report 2003/04.* Paris: UNESCO.

Watkins, F. (2004). 'Evaluation of DFID Development Assistance: Gender Equality and Women's Empowerment. DFID's Experience of Gender Mainstreaming: 1995 to 2004', mimeo. London: DFID.

Whitehead, A. and Lockwood, M. (1999). 'Gendering poverty: a review of six World Bank African Poverty Assessments', *Development and Change* 30(3): 525–55.

Wilson, D. (2003). 'Human Rights: Promoting gender equality in and through education', Background paper for *EFA Global Monitoring Report 2003/04.* Paris: UNESCO.

Wood, K. and Jewkes, R. (1997). 'Violence, rape and sexual coercion: everyday love in a South African township', *Gender and Development* 5: 41–6. Oxford: Oxfam Publishing.

World Bank (2004). *Lessons: 'Scaling up' Successful Efforts to Reduce Poverty.* http://www.worldbank.org/wbi/reducingpoverty/Resources.html (5 January 2005).

Index

access xiv
  conditional cash transfers 102–8
  conflict 81
  global development policy 1
  infrastructure 77–82
  pluralism in the school sector 88
  policies promoting gender equitable schooling
    95, 96
  policy 77–8
  private sector 86
  rights-based approach 30–1
  strategies to promote 100
  subjects 70
  vocational education 75
accountability
  policies promoting gender equitable schooling
    96, 97
  sexual assaults at school 117
achievement
  gender inequality 66–76
  gender patterns in 66–70, 75
  in labour market 75
  primary education 2–3
  single-sex schools 72
  women's empowerment 33, 34
Addis Ababa, Ethiopia 61
adolescent pregnancy
  policies promoting gender equitable schooling
    97
  re-entry after 91, 101
  school policy on 64
  single-sex schools 71
  South Africa 119
adult literacy
  EFA goals 23
  refugee camps 81
advocacy xii, 1, 35
affordability 51, 82
Africa
  child labour 55
  concern for safety of female children 51
  gender-based violence at school 61–3
  structural adjustment 53–4
  see also individual countries
Africa Girls' Education Initiative 132
AFT see Analytical Fast Track
age-dependency ratios 15

agency
  benefits of girls' education 12
  capabilities approach 33, 34
  parental concerns over female education 44–5
  relationship to female education 15–16
  substantive gender equality 25
  see also autonomy; empowerment
agriculture
  benefits of girls' education 10
  demand for female education 55–6
  father migration 54
  HIV/AIDS 48
  seasonal variations 103
Alsop, R. 32–3
alternative education centres 88, 99
American Association of University Women
  60, 66
Analytical Fast Track (AFT) 139
Ansell, N. 70
apprenticeship schemes 74
Arnot, M. 67, 74
Asia
  intersections of exclusion 6–7
  private schools 85
  school costs 82, 83
  see also Central Asia; East Asia; South Asia
aspirations
  gender identities 43
  parental concerns over female education 45
  post-secondary education 73
  subject choice 73, 74
assets, women's empowerment 33
attainment see educational outcomes
attendance
  conditional cash transfers 104
  school costs 84
  strategies to increase 101
Australia
  gender patterns in educational achievement 67
  Gender Responsive Budget Analysis 135
autonomy
  benefits of girls' education 12
  capabilities approach 32–4
  parental concerns over female education 44–5
  relationship to female education 15–16
  single-sex schools 71
  substantive gender equality 25
  see also agency; empowerment
Avalos, B. 76
Azerbaijan 76

backlash 61, 67
Baden, S. 50
Bailey, B. 75
Bamberger, M. 137
Bangladesh
  conditional cash transfers 104, 106, 107–8
  discrimination by teachers 65
  empowerment of adult women 113
  gender patterns in educational achievement 68
  intersections of exclusion 7
  private sector 86
  returns on investment in secondary education 19
Bangladesh Rural Advancement Committee
  (BRAC) 113
Barrientos, A. 103, 105
Basu, A.M. 17
Baudino, C. 65, 67, 73
Beijing Conference *see* World Conference on
  Women
benefits, of girls' education 10–12
Bennell, P. 85, 88
Benson, C. 90
bereavement 103
'best interests', of female children 51
best practice 98–119
bilingual programmes 88–90, 99, 101
birth order 50
Blackmore, J. 67
Blaug, M. 8
Boler, T. 11, 47–8
Bolsa Escola (Brazil) 106
Botswana
  adolescent pregnancy 64, 91
  division of labour at school 64
  fertility rate 14
boys
  adolescent pregnancy 91
  completion rates 4
  decision-making on household resources 51
  discrimination by teachers 65
  empowerment of 119
  gender-based violence at school 116, 117, 119
  gender inequality 2
  gender patterns in achievement 66–70, 75
  out-of-school children 2004 3
  repetition rates 4, 5
  work 42
BRAC *see* Bangladesh Rural Advancement
  Committee
Bray, M. 88
Brazil 104, 106

bridge schools 87–8, 101
Britto, T. 105
budgeting, gender 134–5
bullying 63, 116
Byrne, B. 123, 126, 128

Cambodia 82
Cameroon
  adolescent pregnancy 46
  gender gap at secondary level 77
capabilities approach 30–4, 36, 43–4
CARE 114–15
carers
  children caring for siblings xiii, 50, 58, 111
  of elderly relatives 49, 54
  intergenerational cycle of deprivation 41
Caribbean
  gender disparity in enrolments at primary level 3
  gender patterns in educational achievement 67–8,
    69–70
  out-of-school children 2004 3
  repetition rates 4
  salary inequality 75–6
  school fees 83
  transition rate 4
  vocational education 5
caste systems
  intersections of exclusion 7–8
  Nepal 6
  private sector 86
CCTs *see* conditional cash transfers
CEDAW *see* Convention on the Elimination of All
  Forms of Discrimination Against Women
Central African Republic 46
Central Asia
  conditional cash transfers 104
  school fees 83
Central Europe
  curriculum 66
  salary inequality 76
Chad 46
Chapman, D.W. 132
Charter on the Rights and Welfare of the African
  Child (1990) 27
Chepang (Nepal) 6
child labour
  AIDS/HIV 48
  children caring for siblings xiii, 50, 58, 111
  conditional cash transfers 106
  cost of schooling 82
  demand for girls' education 42–3, 53–4, 55–8

to pay for school 55–6, 57
policies promoting gender equitable schooling 96, 97
in school 64–5
used by teachers 63, 65
child marriage *see* early marriage
child mortality 10, 11–12, 13
child soldiers 80
childcare
children caring for siblings xiii, 50, 58, 111
demand for female education 49–50, 58
empowerment of adult women 111
impact on girls' education xiii
policies promoting gender equitable schooling 96
re-entry policies 91
social dimensions of inequality 43–4
strategies to increase attendance 101
children with disabilities (CWD) 7, 52
children out of school *see* out-of-school children
Chile
conditional cash transfers 104, 106–7
gender patterns in educational achievement 68, 69
salary inequality 75–6
subject choice 73
Chile Solidario (Chile) 106–7
China
gender ideologies 38
intersections of exclusion 7
choice
childcare 49–50
of school 84–90
of subjects 70, 73–5
women's empowerment 32–4
civil rights, human rights 27–8
class xii
intersections of exclusion 6
Nepal 6
private sector 85–6
transition rate 4
see also caste systems
co-educational schools 70–2
Colclough, C. 45, 56, 65, 86
Collard, D. 41
collective action 109–15
community
awareness programmes xiii
involvement in policy 99–100
policies promoting gender equitable schooling 95, 96, 97
completion rates 4, 104
compulsory education 22, 23, 27, 82–4

conditional cash transfers (CCTs) 102–8
conflict 49, 79–81
contraception 11–12
Convention on the Elimination of All Forms of Discrimination Against Women (CEDAW) 26, 27, 28
Convention on the Rights of the Child (CRC) (1989) 26, 27, 28
corporal punishment 63, 116
Costa Rica 68
costs *see* school costs
CRC *see* Convention on the Rights of the Child
cross-sectoral interventions 98
curriculum
empowerment of adult women 114–15
gender-based violence at school 118
gender inequality 43
gender mainstreaming 131
'hidden' 60, 65–6
policies promoting gender equitable schooling 96, 97
CWD *see* children with disabilities

Darfur 81
decision-making, household resource distribution 39–43, 50–1, 82–4, 85
degree level, subject choice 74
DeJong, J. 103, 105
demand for female education 37–58
accessibility 100
conditional cash transfers 102–8
financing 101, 102–8
household-level 12–17
policies promoting gender equitable schooling 96
private education 89
rights-based approach 30
women's empowerment 34
democratic participation 11
Democratic Republic of Congo 49
Department for International Development (DFID) (UK) 129, 130, 137, 139
development 1–19
gender mainstreaming 122–41
human rights 27–8
intergenerational transfers of knowledge 1
rights-based approach 28, 29
DFID *see* Department for International Development
Diop, N. 132–3, 135
disability 7, 52, 80, 96

disasters *see* natural disasters

discrimination *see* gender discrimination

displacement
    conflicts 79–81
    natural disasters 81–2

division of labour
    families 42–3
    gender ideologies 37–9
    gender mainstreaming 124–5
    relationship to demand for female education 53–7
    in school 64–5

domestic labour
    children caring for siblings xiii, 50, 58, 111
    conflict 80
    demand for female education 38–9, 42–3, 53–4, 55–8
    education during conflict 81
    fostering in Africa 57
    gender mainstreaming 124–5

domestic violence 11

donors
    education and development 1
    gender mainstreaming 123–4, 130–2, 136–40

Drèz, J. 15, 17

drop-out rates
    adolescent pregnancy 46, 77, 91
    gender-based violence at school 61
    gender patterns in educational achievement 68
    school costs 84
    strategies to reduce 101

Dunne, M. 91

early childhood care and education (ECCE)
    programmes xiii

early marriage 11–12
    conditional cash transfers 108
    conflicts 79
    demand for female education 45
    policies promoting gender equitable schooling 97
    strategies to promote equality 100

East Asia, repetition rates 4

Eastern Europe
    conditional cash transfers 104
    salary inequality 76
    school fees 83

ECCE *see* early childhood care and education

ECLAC *see* Economic Commission for Latin America and the Caribbean

Economic Commission for Latin America and the Caribbean (ECLAC) 75–6

economic growth 10, 14–15

economic security 95–7

Ecuador, sexual abuse at school 62

education for all (EFA) 2
    gender mainstreaming 131, 139
    goals 2–3, 121–2
    public sector 89
    World Education Conference (WEF) (2000) 22–3

Education Guarantee Scheme (EGS) (India) 113

'education guarantee' schools 88, 113

education workers, empowerment of adult women 109, 110–11

educational environments, rights-based approach 30

educational outcomes
    capabilities approach 31–2
    gender inequality 42–3, 66–76
    learning 66–76
    nutrition 15
    pluralism in the school sector 88
    post-secondary education 73
    rights-based approach 30–1
    subject choice 74
    women's empowerment 33, 34

EFA *see* education for all

elementary education *see* primary education

Eloundou-Enyegue, P.M. 4, 15, 46, 77–8

employment
    demand for female education 53–7
    investment in xii
    policies promoting gender equitable schooling 96, 97
    rates of return on investment in education 8–9, 13, 50–1, 53–4
    relationship to female education 14–15
    see also labour

empowerment
    benefits of girls' education 11
    of boys 119
    capabilities approach 32–4
    conflicts 79
    'feminisation' of HIV/AIDS 48–9
    gender and development 125–6
    length of schooling 13
    rates of return on investment in education 13
    relationship to female education 15–16
    rights-based approach 30–2
    strategies for state action 102, 109–15
    see also agency; autonomy

enrolment
    alternative schools 99
    conditional cash transfers 104, 106
    fostering 57

gender disparity at primary level 3
mother-tongue education 90
nutrition 15
private sector 86
school costs 82–4
single-sex schools 72
strategies to increase 101
transition 4–5, 60, 77–8, 96, 101
Equal Opportunities Commission (EOC) (UK) 74
Ethiopia
child labour 56
demand for female education 45, 54
gender-based violence at school 61
gender patterns in educational achievement 68–9
ethnicity
China 7
gender-based violence at school 117
intersections of exclusion 6, 7–8
mother-tongue education 89–90
Nepal 6
Europe
gender disparity in enrolments at primary level 3
vocational education 5
see also Central Europe; Eastern Europe; South-
eastern Europe
'evaded curriculum' 60, 66
exclusion
of children with disabilities 52
intergenerational cycle of deprivation 40–1
intersections of 6–8

family
benefits of girls' education 10
birth order 50
conditional cash transfers 102–8
demand for female education 44–53
division of labour 37–9, 42–3
HIV/AIDS 48
household resource distribution 39–43, 50–1,
82–4, 85
parental concerns over female education 44–5
policies promoting gender equitable schooling
95–7
returns on investment in education 8–17, 50, 51,
53–4
size 10, 11–12, 50
social dimensions of inequality 43–4
Fast Track Initiative (FTI) 131, 139–40
father migration 54–5
fees 82–4
female genital mutilation 11

Female Secondary Stipend Programme (Bangladesh)
108
female teachers 91–3, 101, 109, 110–15
feminism, gender budgeting 134–5
Fentiman, A. 53, 57
fertility
benefits of girls' education 10, 11–12
rates of returns on investment 13
relationship to female education 14–16
Figueroa, M. 69–70
Folbre, N. 41
food security 48, 96, 97
formal equality 24
fostering 56–7
France
curriculum 65
gender patterns in educational achievement 67, 69
subject choice 73
Fransman, J. 65
free education, enrolment rates 82
freedom, parental concerns over female education
44–5
FTI see Fast Track Initiative
Fuller, B. 14

Gabon 46
GAD see gender and development
gender, definition 25
gender budgeting 134–5
gender and development (GAD) 125–6
gender differentiation 71
gender discrimination
gender ideologies 38–9
gender mainstreaming 123, 126
policies promoting gender equitable schooling 96,
97
subject choice 74–5
by teachers 64–5
see also gender disparity; gender inequality; gender
stereotypes
gender disparity
EFA goals 23
MDG goals 23
rights-based approach 30
gender equality
curriculum 65–6
definitions 122
EFA goals 22–3, 24–5, 122
gender mainstreaming 121–41
intergenerational transfers of knowledge 1
MDGs 22

policy 21–36
rates of return on investment in education 13
relationship to female education 14–15
rights-based approach 28
teachers' role in 63–5
see also gender equity; gender inequality; gender parity
gender equity 25–6
impact of investment in education 16–17
pluralism in the school sector 87–8
policies promoting 95 120
private sector 85
public sector 89
gender gaps
gender patterns in educational achievement 66–70
South Asia 1
sub-Saharan Africa 1
gender identities 37–8
aspirations 43
demand for female education 44–6, 49–50, 53–7
development 125–6
female agency 16
gender mainstreaming 131
gender patterns in educational achievement 69
labour 53–7
marriage 44–6, 49–50
puberty 46–7
gender ideologies 37–8
community involvement in policy 99–100
curriculum 65–6
demand for female education 43–7, 49–50, 51
female agency 16
household resource distribution 42
marriage 44–7, 49–50
meaning of female education 51
puberty 46–7
reproducing society through the education system 60
social dimensions of inequality 43–4
strategies for state action 102
subject choice 73–5
see also social norms
gender inequality
child labour 55–6, 64–5
curriculum 65–6
demand 37–58
demand for femail education 53–7
division of labour 37–9, 42–3, 64–5
education outcomes 42–3
intersections of exclusion 6–8

labour 37–9, 42–3, 53–7, 64–5, 75
learning outcomes 66–76
opportunities 42–3
reproduced through education 51, 60
rights-based approach 30
salary inequality 75–6
school division of labour 64–5
social dimensions of 43–4
supply-side frameworks 59–60
teaching materials 65–6
see also gender discrimination; gender disparity; gender equality
gender intensification 71
gender mainstreaming 2, 121–41
gender parity
EFA goals 22–4, 122
female teachers 91–3
gender mainstreaming 129, 131, 138
teachers 64
see also gender disparity; gender equality; gender equity
Gender Responsive Budget Analysis 134–5
gender roles
community involvement in policy 99–100
curriculum 65–6
see also gender ideologies
gender stereotypes
co-educational schools 71
subject choice 73–5
teaching materials 65–6
gender streaming 72
gender training 130
gender-awareness training 128–9
gender-based violence
at school 61–3, 115–19
rights-based approach 29
strategies for state action 101, 102, 115–19
geographical inequality 6, 7–8, 77
geography, gender ideologies 38–9
Ghana
division of labour at school 64
fostering in Africa 57
gender-based violence at school 61, 62
marriage 46
private sector 86
re-entry after pregnancy 91
girls
completion rates 4
demand for education 37–58
empowerment 30–4
intersections of inequality 6–8

out-of-school children 2004 3
out-performing boys 66–70
policies to promote gender equality 95–119
repetition rates 4, 5
responsibility for siblings xiii, 50, 58, 111
returns on investment in education 9–19
rights-based approach 26–34
supply-side constraints 59–93
transition rate 4–5
work 42
Goetz, A.-M. 127
Greene, C. 50
Grown, C. 13
Guinea 46, 65
Guinea-Bissau 90

Hargreaves, J. 11, 47–8
Harriss-White, B. 86
Hashim, I. 46, 57
HCT see human capital theory
health
benefits of girls' education 10
CEDAW 27
children with disabilities 52
clean water 79
conditional cash transfers 103, 104, 105
conflicts 80
maternal 11–12
policies promoting gender equitable schooling 96, 97
rates of return on investment in education 13
relationship to female education 50
strategies to increase enrolment 101
see also reproductive health
heavily indebted poor countries (HIPCS) 136
Heinsohn, N. 32–3
Herz, B. 1, 10, 12, 91–2, 98
Heward, C. 17
hidden curriculum 60, 65–6
Hill, A.M. 10
HIPCS see heavily indebted poor countries
HIV/AIDS
benefits of girls' education 11
'feminisation' of 47–9
fostering in sub-Saharan Africa 56–7
prevention programmes 115
rape of young girls 62
strategies to increase attendance 101
home economics 65, 70
homosexuality 62
Hoole 137
hospitals, conditional cash transfers 104

hostels, infrastructure 78
households
conditional cash transfers 102–8
costs of education 56
division of labour 42–3
household resource distribution 39–43, 50–1, 82–4, 85
income from child labour 56
policies promoting gender equitable schooling 95–7
human capital theory (HCT) 8–17, 31–2, 43–4, 103
human rights 26–30
Human Rights Watch 61, 62
Hungary 68

ICCPR see International Covenant on Civil and Political Rights
IDPs see internally displaced persons
in-kind transfers 103
incentive programmes xiii
conditional cash transfers 102–8
relationship to demand for female education 58
income
benefits of girls' education 10
from child labour 56
private sector 86
relationship to education 8–9
income shocks, conditional cash transfers 104
India
child labour 56
costs of school 103
demand for female education 45–6, 54, 56
empowerment of women 109–15
gender equality 15
gender inequality in the civil service 127
infrastructure 78
labour 54, 56
marriage 45–6
out-of-school children 2004 3
private sector 86, 87
public sector 87–8
school costs 82
Indian Administrative Service 127
indicators
conditional cash transfers 104
development of xii–xiii, 36
EFA goals 22–6
gender equality 24
impact of investment in education on gender equity 16–17
rights-based approach 30–2

Indonesia 75
inequality
    intersections of 98
    see also gender inequality
infant mortality 13
infrastructure 77–82, 96
institutional transformation 121–41
intergenerational bargain 41
intergenerational transfer
    of assets 47
    benefits of girls' education 10
    demand for female education 10, 15, 50
    of deprivation 40–1, 58
    empowerment of adult women 109
    of knowledge 1
internally displaced persons (IDPs) 81
International Conference Declarations on Gender
    and Education 28–9
International Covenant on Civil and Political
    Rights (ICCPR) 27
International Covenant on Economic, Social and
    Cultural Rights (ICESCR) (1966) 26, 27
International Gay and Lesbian Human Rights
    Commission 62
international law, human rights 26–30
intersections of exclusion 6–8, 98
investment xii
    capabilities approach 31–2
    conditional cash transfers 103–4
    education and development 1
    household decision-making 39–43, 50–1, 82–4, 85
    human capital theory 8–17
    to increase demand for female education 58
    indicators xii–xiii
    interlinkages between sectors 35
    relationship between labour and female education
        53–4
    school costs 84
    secondary education 18–19
    supply-side 59–60
    to support male education 50
    see also returns on investment
Iraq, gender of out-of-school children 2004 3

Jain, D. 124
Jain, S. 109, 111–12
Jamaica 65, 69–70
Jeffery, P. 13–14, 16, 45–6, 51
Jeffery, R. 13–14, 16, 17, 45–6, 51
Jha, J. 89

Kaabwe, E.S.M. 55, 71
Kabeer, N. 14, 17
    gender and development 125
    gender ideologies 38, 39
    household decision-making 40
    intergenerational cycle of deprivation 41
    social dimensions of inequality 43–4
    substantive equality 24
    women's empowerment 32–4
Kane, E. 72
    best practice 98–9
    mother-tongue education 90
    strategies to promote equality 100
Kenya
    adolescent pregnancy 46
    fertility rate 14
    free education 82
King, E. 10
Kingdon, G. 54
Kirk, J. 80
Knodel, J. 53, 54, 56, 77

labour
    demand for female education 53–7
    families 42–3
    gender ideologies 37–9
    gender mainstreaming 124–5
    gendered division of 37–9, 42–3, 53–7, 65–6,
        124–5
    HIV/AIDS 48
    policies promoting gender equitable schooling 95,
        96, 97
    in school 64–5
    social dimensions of inequality 43–4
    subject choice 74–5
    see also child labour; domestic labour; employment
Lange, M.F. 73, 76
language
    bilingual programmes 88–90, 99, 101
    gender patterns in educational achievement 67, 68
    Nepal 6
Latin America
    child labour 55
    out-of-school children 2004 3
    primary enrolments 3
    repetition rates 4
    school fees 83
    transition rate 4
    vocational education 5
Leach, F. 50, 61–3, 91, 115–16
learning styles 71, 72

Leclercq, F. 88
Lee, W. 75
Lesotho 70
Lewin, K. 82, 85
Liang, X. 14
literacy
    adult 23, 81
    EFA goals 23
    empowerment of adult women 110
    gender patterns in educational achievement 67, 68
    HIV/AIDS 48–9
    women with disabilities 52
Lloyd, C. 78
Lockwood, M. 137
Lok Jumbish (India) 110, 111–12, 114

McNay, K. 14, 49
Magno, C. 66
Mahila Samakhya (India) 110, 112–13
Malawi
    adolescent pregnancy 46
    child labour used by teachers 65
    free education 82
    gender-based violence at school 61
Male, J. 72
male privilege
    gender mainstreaming 131
    male under-achievement 69–70
Malhotra, A. 13, 16
marriage
    benefits of girls' education 11–12
    conditional cash transfers 108
    conflicts 79
    demand for female education 44–53
    early 11–12, 45, 79, 97, 100, 108
    impact of investment in education on 17
    policies promoting gender equitable schooling 97
    strategies to promote equality 100
maternal education
    demand for female education 50
    intergenerational transfers of deprivation xiii, 40–1, 58
    level of education of 3
maternal mortality 11–12
mathematics 67, 68, 72
MDGs see Millennium Development Goals
Mehran, G. 44
Mexico 104, 106
Middle East, school fees 83
migration
    fathers 54–5

fostering in Africa 57
    see also displacement
Millennium Development Goals (MDGs) 22–3, 122, 131, 139
Miller, C. 126
Miller, E. 68
mobile schools 101
mobility
    empowerment of adult women 110, 113
    infrastructure 77
monitoring 96
Monterrey Consensus (2002) 139
Moore, K. 40
Morley, Samuel 104
Moser, C. 127
mother-tongue education 88–90, 99, 101
mothers
    conditional cash transfers to 105
    right to continue schooling 29
    see also maternal education
motivation, post-secondary education 73
Mozambique 46, 90
Mturi, A.J. 56
Murthi, M. 12

NASSPE see National Association for Single Sex Public Education
National Association for Single Sex Public Education (NASSPE) 71
national identities 89–90
national machineries 123, 127–8
national net enrolment ratio (NER) 6
natural disasters 81–2
    Bangladesh 7
    displacement 79
Nepal 6, 80
NER see national net enrolment ratio
NGOs see non-governmental organisations
Nieuwenhuys, O. 56
Niger 90
Nigeria 72
non-governmental organisations (NGOs)
    empowerment of adult women 113–15
    private schools 85
non-state providers 85
normative framework 31–2
North Africa
    gender ideologies 38
    school fees 83
numeracy, EFA goals 23
Nussbaum, M. 31

GENDER IN PRIMARY AND SECONDARY EDUCATION

nutrition
 conditional cash transfers 105
 investment in xii
 policies promoting gender equitable schooling 97
 relationship to female education 15, 50
 strategies to increase enrolment 101

Odora-Hoppers, C. 124, 132
OECD-DAC 121, 137–8
opportunities, gender inequality 42–3, 44
orphans
 fostering in sub-Saharan Africa 56–7
 HIV/AIDS 47
out-of-school children 3
 conflicts 80
 intra-regional variation 6
 policies promoting gender equitable schooling 96
 transitional schooling 87–8
outcomes see educational outcomes
Oxaal, Z. 9, 56

Pacific, repetition rates 4
Pakistan
 child labour 55
 infrastructure 78
 private sector 86, 89
 single-sex schools 72, 78
Pande, R. 13, 16
Parent-Teacher Associations 81
parental education
 father migration 54–5
 intergenerational transfers of deprivation 40–1, 58
 relationship to demand for female education 50
 see also maternal education
parents
 'best interests' of female children 51
 concerns over female education 44–6, 65
 cost of schooling 82–4
 demand for female education 12–17, 37–58, 65
 education during conflict 80
 gender-based violence at school 116
 involvement in school 101
 policies promoting gender equitable schooling 96
 private schools 85
 single-sex schools 71
participation
 conflict 81
 current levels 35
 empowerment of adult women 109–15
 gender mainstreaming 131

rights-based approach 30
 strategies to increase attendance 101
pastoralism 56
patriarchy
 gender ideologies 38–9
 impact of investment in education on gender equity 16, 17
peer support networks 101
Philippines 82
Phipps, A. 67, 74
Pietila, H. 124
Pilon, M. 57
PISA see Programme for International Student Assessment
Poland 76
policy xi–xii
 capabilities approach 31–2
 community involvement in 99–100
 cross-sectoral interventions 98
 empowerment of women 32
 gender equality 21–36
 gender equity in access 1
 gender inequality 39
 gender mainstreaming 121–41
 gender-neutral 98–9
 indicators xii–xiii
 infrastructure 77–82
 localised interventions 99
 multiple interventions 98–9
 post-conflict reconstruction 81
 private education 88–9
 promoting gender equitable schooling 95–120
 rates of return on investment in education 8–17
 re-entry after pregnancy 91
 social norms 102–19
 strategies to increase transition rates 101–19
 supply 59, 77–93
political rights 27–8
politics, gender mainstreaming 131
post-secondary education, subject choice 73–4
poverty
 Bangladesh 7
 China 7
 conditional cash transfers 102–8
 gender mainstreaming 136–7
 human rights 27–8
 intergenerational transfer of xiii, 40–1, 58
 intersections of exclusion 6–7
 policies promoting gender equitable schooling 95–7
 private schools 85–6
poverty reduction strategies (PRS) 136–40

162

poverty reduction strategy papers (PRSPs) 131, 136–7, 138, 139–40
power relations
  capabilities approach 32–4
  'feminisation' of HIV/AIDS 48
  gender-based violence at school 117
  gender mainstreaming 124
  pregnancy
    adolescent 46, 64, 71, 91, 97, 101, 119
    demand for female education 44–5, 49–50, 58
    parental fear of 51
    policies promoting gender equitable schooling 97
    re-entry policies 29, 91, 101
    school drop-outs 77
    sexual violence in conflict 80
    single-sex schools 71
    social dimensions of inequality 43–4
    see also childcare
pregnancy-related deaths 11–12
primary education
  achievements 2–3
  compulsory 22, 23, 27, 82–4
  conditional cash transfers 107
  countries that charge for 83
  demand for 12–17
  and development 1
  EFA goals 22, 23
  female teachers 92
  free 22, 23, 27
  gender parity goals 2005 2–3
  infrastructure 77, 78
  MDG goals 23
  private schools 85, 86
  rates of return on investment in education 13, 19
  repetition rate 4
  rights-based approach 27
  strategies to increase attendance 101
  transition from 4–5, 60, 77–8, 96, 101
Primary Education Stipend Programme (Bangladesh) 107
private sector 84–90
PROBE see Public Report on Basic Education
productivity, human capital theory 8–17
Programme for International Student Assessment (PISA) 74
Progresa (Mexico) 106
PRS see poverty reduction strategies
PRSPs see poverty reduction strategy papers
psycho-social care 96, 97

puberty
  gender ideology 46–7
  single-sex schools 71
Public Report on Basic Education (PROBE) 86
public sector
  fragmentation 87–8
  quality 84, 85–6, 87–8
  school choice 84–5
punishment
  gender-based violence at school 63, 116, 117
  male under-achievement 70

quality
  policies promoting gender equitable schooling 96, 97
  private schooling 88–9
  public sector 84, 85–6, 87–8

Ramachandran, V. 88, 97, 109
Ramagoshi, M. 117
rape
  gender-based violence at school 61–3, 115–16
  by teachers 63–4
rates of return see returns on investment
Razavi, S. 126
RBA see rights-based approach
re-entry policies 91, 101
'readiness' for school 53
refugee camps 81
religion
  gender ideologies 38
  intersections of exclusion 7–8
remedial education 101
remote areas
  Bangladesh 7
  China 7
  infrastructure 77, 78
  intra-regional variation 6
repetition 4
  father migration 54
  gender patterns in educational achievement 69
  primary schools 4
  secondary schools 5
reproductive health
  benefits of girls' education 11–12
  demand for female education 58
  'feminisation' of HIV/AIDS 47–9
  impact on girls' education xiii
  rights-based approach 28, 29
residential schools
  India 111–12

infrastructure 78
strategies to increase enrolment 101
resources
  conflicts 79
  HIV/AIDS 47
  household decision-making 39–43, 50–1, 82–4, 85
  intergenerational bargain 41
  school costs 82–4
  women's empowerment 33, 34
respectability, gender ideology 51
returns on investment
  capabilities approach 31–2
  gender equity 16–17
  household decision-making 39–43, 50–1, 82–4, 85
  human capital theory 8–17
  labour 53–4
  length of schooling 13
  link to investment in other forms of gender
equality 18
  nutrition 15
  pathways 12–16
  private 8–9
  public 9–17
  school costs 84
  secondary education 18–19
  supporting family finances 50
  thresholds 13
rights 26–34
  gender mainstreaming 122
  policies promoting gender equitable schooling 96
  public sector 89
  school choice 84
rights-based approach (RBA) 26–34
rites of passage 46–7
Romania 66, 76
Rose, P. 22, 50, 51, 54
  costs of education 56
  gender mainstreaming 131, 139, 140
  school costs 82
Rosenberg 136
rural areas
  conditional cash transfers 107
  infrastructure 77, 78
  intersections of exclusion 6
Rwanda 132–3

safety
  education during conflict 81
  empowerment of adult women 111, 113
  female teachers 92–3
  gender-based violence at school 117–18

infrastructure 77–8
parental concerns 51
policies promoting gender equitable schooling 96, 97
strategies for state action 101, 102, 115–19
SAHE see Society for the Advancement of Education
Saith, R. 86
salaries see income; wages
Al-Samarrai, S. 54, 56
Sarraf, F. 134, 135
Sathar, Z.A. 11, 53
Save the Children 45, 80
scholarships 84, 101
school costs 82–4
  accessibility 100
  child labour 56
  conditional cash transfers 103
  policies promoting gender equitable schooling 96, 97
  strategies to increase enrolment 101
  strategies to promote equality 100
schooling see education
schooling for subordination hypothesis 60
schools
  bilingual programmes 88–90, 99, 101
  calendar 101
  choice of 84–90
  conditional cash transfers 104
  conflicts 79–81
  cost of building 82
  costs 103
  curriculum 65–6
  demand 37–58
  division of labour 64–5
  fees 82–4
  fragmentation 87–8
  gender-based violence at 61–3, 115–19
  gender inequality in teaching materials 65–6
  gender patterns in educational achievement 66–70
  governance 96
  infrastructure 77–82
  management of xiv
  non-formal 87–8
  pluralism 87–8
  policies promoting gender equitable schooling 95, 96, 97
  private sector 84–90
  public sector 84–6, 87–8
  re-entry after pregnancy 91, 101

reform 59
refugee camps 81
sexual violence by teachers 63–4
single-sex 70–2, 78, 101
strategies to increase enrolment 101
supply 59–93
textbooks 82, 100, 101, 103
see also primary education; school costs; secondary education
seasonal variations 103
secondary education
    adolescent pregnancy 46, 77
    conditional cash transfers 108
    gender-based violence at 61–2
    gender gap 1
    gender parity goals 2005 3
    infrastructure 77–8
    MDG goals 23
    repetition rate 5
    returns on investment 13, 18–19
    single-sex 71
    strategies to increase transition rates 101
    transition to 4–5, 60, 77–8, 96, 101
sector wide approaches (SWAps) 131, 137–8, 139–40
self-perception 39, 43
Sen, A. 15, 17, 31
Sewell, T. 69, 70
sex education 91
sex work 46, 49, 63, 80
sexual abuse
    policies promoting gender equitable schooling 96, 97
    rights-based approach 29
sexual harassment
    rights-based approach 29
    strategies for state action 102, 115–19
sexual violence
    conflict 79, 80
    curriculum 118
    HIV/AIDS 48, 49
    parental concerns about female education 51
    in school 61–3, 115–19
    by teachers 63–4
sexuality
    control of 44
    'feminisation' of HIV/AIDS 47–9
    gender-based violence at school 62
    puberty 46–7, 71
Shiksha Karmi (India) 110
Sibbons, M. 138

single-sex classrooms 72
single-sex schools 70–2, 78, 101
social development
    relationship to female education 14–15
    rights-based approach 28
social groups, intersections of exclusion 5–8
social norms
    'best interests' of female children 51
    community involvement in policy 99–100
    curriculum 65–6
    demand for female education 37–9
    education outcomes 42–3
    empowerment of adult women 109–15
    female agency 15–16
    gender and development 125–6
    gender mainstreaming 123, 131
    household resource distribution 39–42
    parental concerns over female education 44–5
    policies promoting gender equitable schooling 97
    self-perceptions 43
    social dimensions of inequality 43–4
    strategies for state action 102
    teachers 63–5
    see also gender ideologies
Society for the Advancement of Education (SAHE) 114
son-preference 38
South Africa
    adolescent pregnancy 46
    conditional cash transfers 104
    gender-based violence at school 61, 62, 63, 115, 117–19
    home economics 70
South Asia
    best practice 98
    concern for safety of female children 51
    empowerment of adult women 109–15
    gender gap 1
    gender ideologies 38, 49
    gender parity goals 2005 3
    private sector 86, 88–9
    repetition rates 4
    vocational education 5
South Korea 38
South-eastern Europe, curriculum 66
Southern Africa, child labour 56
Sperling, G. 1, 10–11, 12, 91–2, 98
Sri Lanka 38
state
    capabilities approach 31
    gender mainstreaming 126–7

policies promoting gender equitable schooling 95, 96, 97
strategies for action 101–19
stationery, costs 82
stipends 84, 101, 107–8
structural adjustment 53–4
sub-Saharan Africa
    best practice 98
    female teachers 92
    fostering 56–7
    free education 82
    gender gap 1
    gender parity goals 2005 3
    HIV/AIDS 47
    repetition rates 4, 5
    school fees 83
    sexual violence by teachers 63
    single-sex schools 71
    vocational education 5
subjects, choice of 70, 73–5
Subrahmanian, R. 22, 39, 50, 51, 89, 131, 140
substantive equality 24–5
Sudan 81
supervision, male under-achievement 69–70
supply 59–93
    policy 77–93
    rights-based approach 30
    women's empowerment 34
SWAps see sector wide approaches
Swaziland, father migration 54–5

Tabor, S. 102
Taiwan 38, 50
Tansel, A. 53, 56, 77
Tanzania 4, 82
teachers
    attitudes of 43
    conditions of work 101
    conflicts 79, 81
    empowerment of adult women 109, 110–15
    female 91–3, 101, 109, 110–15
    gender-based violence at school 61–3, 115–16, 117
gender equality 29
    gender parity of 64
    localised recruitment 99
    male under-achievement 70
    mother-tongue education 90
    policies promoting gender equitable schooling 96, 97
    private sector 86

re-entry after pregnancy 91
refugee camps 81
role in gender equality 63–5
sexual assault by 61, 62
strategies to increase attendance 101
training 29, 93
use of child labour 63, 65
teaching materials
    costs 82, 100
    gender inequality in 65–6
    strategies to increase attendance 101
Tembon, M. 51, 56
tertiary education
    data on 5
    female unemployment 75–6
    gender gap 1
    returns on investment 13
    subject choice 73–4
textbooks
    costs 82, 100
    in-kind transfers 103
    strategies to increase attendance 101
Thailand 54
Thakali (Nepal) 6
Thakur 127
thresholds 13
Tilak, J.B.G. 103
Togo
    fostering 57
    gender patterns in educational achievement 69
    salary inequality 76
    subject choice 73
toilets 78–9, 96, 101
Tomasevski, K. 82, 83, 84
training
    empowerment of adult women 111
    gender 130
    gender stereotyping 74
    gender-awareness 128–9
transactional sex 46, 49, 63, 80
transition countries
    curriculum 66
    salary inequality 76
transition from primary to secondary education 4–5
    infrastructure 77–8
    policies promoting gender equitable schooling 96
    strategies to increase rates 101
    supply-side frameworks 60
transitional schooling 87–8, 101
transport 101

Udaan (India) 114–15
UDHR *see* Universal Declaration of Human Rights
UEE *see* universal elementary education
Uganda
 adolescent pregnancy 46
 free education 82
 single-sex schools 72
Ukraine 76
UN *see* United Nations
unemployment
 conditional cash transfers 103
 gender inequality 75–6
UNESCO *see* United Nations Children's Fund
UNGEI *see* United Nations Girls' Education Initiative
UNICEF *see* United Nations Children's Fund
uniforms
 costs 82, 100
 in-kind transfers 103
United Kingdom
 gender mainstreaming 129, 130
 gender patterns in educational achievement 67, 69
 subject choice 73–4
United Nations (UN)
 gender mainstreaming 121, 123, 124
 HIV/AIDS 49
 Millennium Project 10, 49, 82
 rights-based approach 26–8
 school fees 82
United Nations Children's Fund (UNICEF) 2, 98
United Nations Commission on the Status of Women 123
United Nations Educational, Scientific and Cultural Organisation (UNESCO)
 child labour 55
 children with disabilities 52
 Convention against Discrimination in Education (1960) 27
 early marriage 45
 education during conflict 80
 female teachers 92
 gender patterns in educational achievement 68–9
 Global Monitoring Report on Education for All (2004) 5
 Global Monitoring Report on Education for All (2005) 2–3
 Global Monitoring Report on Education for All (2007) 3, 4
 tertiary education 5

United Nations Girls' Education Initiative (UNGEI) 132, 139–40
United Nations International Conference on Population and Development (Cairo 1994) 28
United States, single-sex schools 71
Universal Declaration of Human Rights (UDHR) 27
universal elementary education (UEE) 1
universal primary education (UPE) 132, 139
Unterhalter, E. 31–2, 139–40
UPE *see* universal primary education
Uttar Pradesh, India 45–6

Vickers, J. 124
Vienna Conference *see* World Conference on Human Rights
Vietnam 82
violence
 gender-based violence at school 61–3, 115–19
 policies promoting gender equitable schooling 96
 strategies for state action 115–19
vocational education
 access to 75
 data on 5
 policies promoting gender equitable schooling 96, 97
 women teachers 114

wages
 gender inequality 75–6
 policies promoting gender equitable schooling 96, 97
 rates of return on investment in education 13
 relationship to education 8–9
water supply
 infrastructure 78–9
 policies promoting gender equitable schooling 96, 97
 strategies to increase attendance 101
Watkins, F. 130
WEF *see* World Education Forum
West Asia
 gender parity goals 2005 3
 repetition rates 4
Whitehead, A. 137
WID *see* women in development
Wilson, D. 26, 29–30, 45
women
 empowerment of 11, 109–15
 rights-based approach 28
 self-perceptions 39, 43
women in development (WID) movement 124–5

Women's Residential Institute for Training and Education (WRITE) 111

World Bank
Ecuador 62
gender mainstreaming 131, 132, 137
rates of return on investment in education 10

World Conference on Education for All (Jomtien 1990) 22

World Conference on Human Rights (Vienna 1993) 28

World Conference on Women (Beijing 1995) 28

World Education Forum (WEF) (Dakar 2000) , 139

World Health Organisation (WHO) 52

World Summit for Social Development (Copenhagen 1995) 28

WRITE *see* Women's Residential Institute for Training and Education

Yemen 3

Zambia 46

Zimbabwe 14, 61, 62